Past Masters
General Editor Keith Thomas

Vico

Past Masters

AQUINAS Anthony Kenny
ARISTOTLE Jonathan Barnes
BACH Denis Arnold
FRANCIS BACON Anthony Quinton
BAYLE Elisabeth Labrousse
BERGSON Leszek Kolakowski
BERKELEY J. O. Urmson
THE BUDDHA Michael Carrithers
BURKE C. B. Macpherson
CARLYLE A. L. Le Quesne
CERVANTES P. E. Russell
CHAUCER George Kane
CLAUSEWITZ Michael Howard
COBBETT Raymond Williams
COLERIDGE Richard Holmes
CONFUCIUS Raymond Dawson
DANTE George Holmes
DARWIN Jonathan Howard
DIDEROT Peter France
GEORGE ELIOT Rosemary Ashton
ENGELS Terrell Carver
GALILEO Stillman Drake
GIBBON J. W. Burrow
GOETHE T. J. Reed
HEGEL Peter Singer

HOMER Jasper Griffin
HUME A. J. Ayer
JESUS Humphrey Carpenter
KANT Roger Scruton
LAMARCK L. J. Jordanova
LEIBNIZ G. MacDonald Ross
LOCKE John Dunn
MACHIAVELLI Quentin Skinner
MARX Peter Singer
MENDEL Vitezslav Orel
MILL William Thomas
MONTAIGNE Peter Burke
THOMAS MORE Anthony Kenny
WILLIAM MORRIS Peter Stansky
MUHAMMAD Michael Cook
NEWMAN Owen Chadwick
PASCAL Alban Krailsheimer
PETRARCH Nicholas Mann
PLATO R. M. Hare
PROUST Derwent May
RUSKIN George P. Landow
ADAM SMITH D. D. Raphael
TOLSTOY Henry Gifford
VICO Peter Burke
WYCLIF Anthony Kenny

Forthcoming

AUGUSTINE Henry Chadwick
BAGEHOT H. C. G. Matthew
BENTHAM John Dinwiddy
JOSEPH BUTLER R. G. Frey
COPERNICUS Owen Gingerich
DESCARTES Tom Sorell
DISRAELI John Vincent
ERASMUS John McConica
GODWIN Alan Ryan
HERZEN Aileen Kelly
JEFFERSON Jack P. Greene
JOHNSON Pat Rogers
KIERKEGAARD Patrick Gardiner
LEONARDO E. H. Gombrich
LINNAEUS W. T. Stearn

MALTHUS Donald Winch
MONTESQUIEU Judith Shklar
NEWTON P. M. Rattansi
ROUSSEAU Robert Wokler
RUSSELL John G. Slater
SHAKESPEARE Germaine Greer
SOCRATES Bernard Williams
SPINOZA Roger Scruton
TOCQUEVILLE Larry Siedentop
VIRGIL Jasper Griffin
MARY WOLLSTONECRAFT
  William St Clair

and others

Peter Burke

Vico

Oxford   New York
OXFORD UNIVERSITY PRESS
1985

Oxford University Press, Walton Street, Oxford OX2 6DP

Oxford New York Toronto
Delhi Bombay Calcutta Madras Karachi
Kuala Lumpur Singapore Hong Kong Tokyo
Nairobi Dar es Salaam Cape Town
Melbourne Auckland

and associated companies in
Beirut Berlin Ibadan Mexico City Nicosia

Oxford is a trade mark of Oxford University Press

British Library Cataloguing in Publication Data
Burke, Peter
Vico.—(Past Masters)
1. Vico, Giambattista
I. Title   II. Series
195   B3583
ISBN 0–19–287619–8
ISBN 0–19–287618–X pbk

Library of Congress Cataloging in Publication Data
Burke, Peter.
Vico.
(Past masters)
Bibliography: p.
Includes index.
1. Vico, Giambattista, 1668–1744.   I. Title.
II. Series.
B3583.B84 1985   195   84–29628
ISBN 0–19–287619–8
ISBN 0–19–287618–X (pbk.)

Set by Grove Graphics
Printed in Great Britain by St. Edmundsbury Press Ltd.
Bury St. Edmunds, Suffolk

Contents

For
Arnaldo Momigliano

Acknowledgements

Extracts from *The New Science of Giambattista Vico: Unabridged Translation of the Third Edition (1744) with the addition of 'Practice of the New Science'*, translated by Thomas Goddard Bergin and Max Harold Fisch (Copyright 1948 by Cornell University), are included by kind permission of the publisher, Cornell University Press.

I should like to thank my friend and colleague Anthony Pagden for his comments on a draft of Chapter 3, and Vivian Salmon for reading the section on language.

Note on references and abbreviations

References to the *New Science* (N) are given by the paragraphs (as numbered by the Italian editor, Fausto Nicolini), a system which has been followed in most subsequent editions and translations. Passages cited from the *Autobiography* (A) and from the second edition of the *New Science* (N2) follow the translation by Thomas Bergin and Max Fisch. Translations from *The Ancient Wisdom of the Italians* (W) and the first edition of the *New Science* (N) use the version by Leo Pompa. Translations from *The Study Methods of Our Time* follow that by Elio Gianturco. The remaining translations are my own.

1 The myth of Vico

Giambattista Vico (1668–1744) is a thinker who has inspired, since his death, an extraordinary enthusiasm in the most diverse readers, whether they are radicals or conservatives, poets or lawyers, philosophers or historians. The enthusiasts range from Jules Michelet to Friedrich von Savigny, from Karl Marx to Benedetto Croce, from Matthew Arnold to James Joyce. Many of them have viewed him as a man born out of his time, a precursor, 'neither more nor less than the nineteenth century in embryo' as the Italian philosopher Croce (1866–1952) once put it. He has been regarded as the founder—unrecognized by his contemporaries—of the philosophy of history or even of social science, and as a man whose ideas anticipated such later intellectual movements as pragmatism, historicism, existentialism, and structuralism. The English philosopher R. G. Collingwood (1889–1943) once described him as 'too far ahead of his time to have very much immediate influence', while Isaiah Berlin has declared that 'when Vico said that he was a solitary traveller in territory hitherto traversed by no one, this often repeated classical cliché for once expressed the literal truth'.

My own view is that these claims and descriptions are somewhat exaggerated, and that they form part of what might reasonably be called the 'myth' of Vico in the sense of a stylized interpretation of his career in dramatic terms—a tragicomedy of errors or misunderstanding which is put right in the end, although rather too late for the hero. I believe that this interpretation is seriously misleading. It has torn Vico from his context, separating him from the

1

cultural and social milieu in which he developed, the city of Naples in the late seventeenth century. It has also detached Vico from his wider intellectual tradition, that of the humanist republic of letters and in particular the lawyers who were still among its leading citizens. Although Vico was a profoundly original thinker, he still owed a great deal to that milieu and to that tradition, both of which will be discussed in the next chapter.

It is true that Vico was a prophet without honour in his own country in his own day, dismissed as obscure, speculative, unsound (*stravagante*, as the Italians put it), or even slightly mad. His contemporary and fellow-citizen, the great historian Pietro Giannone (1676–1748), once wrote that there was no one in Naples fuller of fantasies and visions than Vico, a remark which was certainly not intended as a compliment. Vico was aware of what others were thinking, and felt himself to be, as he put it, 'a foreigner in his own country' (*straniero nella sua patria*).

He was an outsider. And yet, forty years after his death, a cult of Vico grew up in Naples. Forty years after that, he was translated into French and German, and his ideas became fashionable in certain intellectual circles. A century or so after his death, he began to be accepted by Italian philosophers and assimilated into their tradition. Two centuries after his death, his major work, the *New Science*, was finally translated into English. The tercentenary of Vico's birth, in 1968, was marked by large international conferences in his honour. Two institutes for 'Vico studies' and a journal devoted to him have been founded within the last few years.

This shift from neglect on the part of contemporaries to enthusiasm on the part of posterity—a section of post-erity at any rate—is extremely striking, and it demands explanation. Why have people come to feel such enthusiasm for this early eighteenth-century Neapolitan? What exactly do they see in him and in his books?

They do not always see the same things, and so it may be useful to approach Vico's intellectual personality by way of a brief history of his posthumous reputation. The story begins in Naples in the late eighteenth century with an attempt to reform the law, part of an international movement associated with the Enlightenment. Law had been one of Vico's central concerns. He did not himself advocate legal reform, but he did point out—like his contemporary Montesquieu—that different types of State or society necessarily give rise to different types of law; and from this premise it could be argued that when society changes, as Naples and other parts of Europe were changing in the later eighteenth century, the law must be modified to bring it into line. A number of Neapolitans who argued in this way, who supported the French Revolution, and who wished to abolish the power and privileges of the local barons, were also admirers of Vico. After they were forced into exile in 1799, these reformers began to spread the knowledge of Vico's ideas in Milan, Paris, and elsewhere. However, it was not necessary to be a supporter of the principles of 1789 in order to take an interest in what Vico had to say about legal evolution. Friedrich Karl von Savigny (1779–1861), for example, the founder of the German 'historical school' of law and a conservative who opposed legal reform on the grounds that a nation's law was the natural product of its past, saw Vico as a predecessor and as a misunderstood genius.

Another central interest of Vico's was poetry. A poet himself, he argued that different kinds of poetry, like different kinds of law, were appropriate to different societies, and that primitive men were necessarily poets because they possessed strong imaginations which compensated for the weakness of their reason. It was perhaps this argument

3

which led a local intellectual to give a copy of Vico's *New Science* to the German poet Johann Wolfgang von Goethe (1749–1832) on his visit to Naples in 1787. Goethe browsed through the book without being particularly impressed, any more than his friend the writer Johann Gottfried Herder (1744–1803) had been, or Herder's friend the philosopher J. G. Hamann (1730–88), who had taken a look at Vico's work ten years earlier. They all found him obscure and did not notice the similarities between his ideas and their own, at least not at first. Yet the thoughts expressed by Herder and his friends in their reaction against the dominance of French classical ideals were in some ways close to Vico's. Like him, they believed in the primacy of poetry in the early development of both individuals and nations.

It was in the next generation, in the early nineteenth century, that German intellectuals began to take Vico seriously, when it was noticed that he had anticipated the apparently revolutionary reinterpretations of the classical past recently put forward by two leading scholars, Wolf and Niebuhr. Friedrich August Wolf (1759–1824) had made his reputation by arguing that Homer had not written either the *Iliad* or the *Odyssey* but that these poems were oral compositions which were written down at a later date and in a modified form. Barthold Georg Niebuhr (1776–1831) owed his fame to an equally dramatic challenge to accepted views of antiquity. Niebuhr argued that the early history of Rome was not so much history as myth, that it was essentially a paraphrase of lost epics or ballads similar to those which had survived from medieval Germany and Denmark; it was this suggestion which inspired Macaulay to reconstruct what he called the 'lays of ancient Rome'. After these scholarly theories had been debated for some time, it was noticed that Vico had come to similar conclusions some seventy or eighty years earlier, and that he had followed a similar comparative method. Wolf and

Niebuhr seem to have been unaware of Vico's work until their own had been published. However, the controversy over their originality spread Vico's fame not only in Germany, where a translation of the *New Science* was published in 1822, but in England and France as well.

In England, the poet and critic Samuel Taylor Coleridge (1772–1834), who had been introduced to Vico's ideas by an Italian exile, was deeply impressed by his emphasis on the power of the imagination, a subject on which Coleridge himself had so much to say. Thomas Arnold (1795–1842), who was a classical scholar before he became headmaster of Rugby School, was converted to the reinterpretation of early Roman history offered by Vico and Niebuhr. He called the *New Science* 'so profound and striking that the little celebrity which it has attained out of Italy is one of the most remarkable facts of literary history'. His son Matthew Arnold (1822–88) was also an admirer of Vico, whom he mentions in his lectures and echoes in his poetry. Lines such as 'Time may restore us in its course', or 'And centuries came and ran their course' would seem to be making reference to Vico's theory of the cyclical movement of history, the *corso* and *ricorso* (below, p. 56).

In France, another Italian exile introduced the romantic historian Jules Michelet (1798–1874) to Vico's ideas. Michelet, who was still in his twenties, immediately decided to make this 'prophet', as he called him, better known by translating selections from his work. What particularly excited Michelet was Vico's emphasis on the creativity of peoples as opposed to so-called 'great men'. As he wrote in his vividly metaphorical way: 'I was born from Vico'; 'I was seized by a frenzy caught from Vico.' Michelet's rather free translation appeared in 1827, to be followed by another French version in 1844. Vico became quite fashionable in some French circles in the middle of the nineteenth century. At a time of romantic enthusiasm for the people and of interest in the 'spirit of the age', the moment was right for assimilating Vico into French culture.

On the other hand, the deliberately unromantic 'positivists', who wanted to make history and 'sociology'—a term which they were the first to employ—into sciences on the model of physics or zoology, praised Vico for his interest in the laws of historical evolution, although they also criticized him for being too speculative and not sufficiently concerned with collecting facts. Karl Marx, who had a good deal in common with the positivists, also read Vico, and in the 1860s recommended the *New Science* to one of his correspondents as a book containing 'many a gleam of genius'. No doubt he thought of Vico as a protomarxist, and there are indeed interesting parallels between the ideas of the two thinkers, notably in the importance they attach to social conflict in history and the unimportance of 'great men'.

There was even more interest in Vico among European intellectuals at the time of what has been called the 'revolt against positivism' in the later nineteenth century. Vico's distinction between the world of nature, which we can know only from outside, and the world of men in society, which we know from within because we have in a sense created it ourselves, appealed to those who were resisting the attempts of the 'social scientists' to study human beings as if they were objects. It appealed, for example, to the German philosopher Wilhelm Dilthey (1833–1911), who called the *New Science* 'one of the greatest triumphs of modern thought'. It also appealed to Benedetto Croce, who read the *New Science* in the 1890s and in 1911 published a study of it which remains the most important and the most influential contribution to the subject. This study was translated into English without delay by R. G. Collingwood. Collingwood is often described as a disciple of Croce, but he liked to say that it was Vico who had influenced him more than anyone else. So far as the English-speaking world is concerned, Vico's appearance on the intellectual map probably owes more to Collingwood than to any other individual, apart from the American scholars Bergin and Fisch who translated the *New Science* into English—at long last—in the 1940s.

Like Dilthey and Croce, Collingwood was particularly interested in Vico's contrast between the methods to be employed in the study of nature and the study of man. However, some writers and thinkers of the early twentieth century found Vico fascinating for quite different reasons, notably for his view of myth as concrete thought and of an age of myth as a necessary stage in the intellectual evolution of the human race. The German philosopher Ernst Cassirer (1874–1945), for example, was inspired by Vico, whose book he read in his student days, to devote much of his life to the study of myths and other 'symbolic forms', as he called them. Again, Erich Auerbach (1892–1957), one of the most influential literary critics of the twentieth century, was a great admirer of the *New Science*, of which he made a second German translation. For Auerbach it was Vico's view of the history of culture which was most inspiring, particularly the idea that different aesthetic values have been dominant in different periods, and necessarily so.

As for James Joyce (1882–1941), who made the discovery of the *New Science* when he was living in Trieste and read it in Italian, he was fascinated by Vico's views on myth, on metaphor, on Homer, on language, on psychology, and much else besides. 'My imagination grows when I read Vico', Joyce once confessed, 'as it doesn't when I read Freud or Jung.' He was particularly interested in Vico's interpretation of history in terms of cycles, 'vicous cicles' as they are called in *Finnegans Wake*.

Not only philosophers, critics, and imaginative writers

but social scientists as well have been inspired and excited by Vico: the economist Joseph Schumpeter (1883–1950), for example, who called Vico 'one of the greatest thinkers to be found in any age in the field of the social sciences'. Indeed, since the Second World War there has been something of a Vico revival, and he has come at last to be recognized as a major figure in the history of European thought, a 'past master'. Some philosophers, critics, psychologists, and even geographers would describe themselves as 'Vichians' in the way that others describe themselves as Marxists. As mentioned previously, some enthusiasts go so far as to see Vico as a precursor of psychoanalysis, existentialism, structuralism, and other contemporary intellectual movements.

However, the history of Vico's changing reputation should warn us against taking these assessments too literally or too seriously. In every age, men tend to re-create their predecessors in their own image, and Vico has been viewed in turn, as we have just seen, as a revolutionary, a reactionary, a romantic, a positivist, an anti-positivist, and so on. The myth of the forerunner, the St John the Baptist, remains an extremely powerful one in the Western cultural tradition. Vico seems to lend himself to this diversity of interpretation more readily than other major thinkers. This is due in part to the obscurity or ambiguity of certain important passages in his work (an ambiguity which seems to have harmed him in his own time but benefited him in the long term), and in part to the diversity of his own interests and the intellectual traditions on which he drew. He was a poet and a lawyer, a platonist and a baconian rolled into one. Add to this the fact that he left some of his most important ideas undeveloped, statues in the stone which others could excavate and polish after their own fashion, and it should not be difficult to account for his appeal to very different kinds of people.

Indeed, he deserves to appeal to a variety of readers, now as in the past, for two main reasons. In the first place, we should read the *New Science*, and Vico's other works, as literature. They express a vision of the past which has the sublimity and the imaginative power of the poems of William Blake, another creator of a memorable private mythology. We should read these works in the second place because Vico grappled in an original and constructive way with some fundamental problems in the study of humanity, problems which we are still far from having solved. Is there a pattern in history? Is human nature the same everywhere? If not, in what ways does it differ from one region or period to another? How and why does social change occur? As long as we remain concerned with questions such as these, Vico's reflections will not lack contemporary relevance. His comparative approach, his refusal to be confined within any one discipline, and the imaginative effort he made to understand other cultures all compel admiration and deserve to be emulated, so far as we are able to do so. In an age when the split between the literary and the scientific approaches to the understanding of society is widening into a chasm, there is much for us to learn from Vico.

However, the fact that we can and should learn from him does not entitle us to treat him as a 'modern' man who just happened to be born out of his time. Whether he liked it or not—and he found much to criticize in the age he lived in—Vico belonged to the culture of late seventeenth-century Naples, as the next chapter attempts to demonstrate.

2 Vico's intellectual development

In studying Vico's milieu and his intellectual development, we are fortunate in the survival of a source so rich and
so relevant as the autobiography which he published in
1728. This is in fact one of the very first autobiographies to
be organized around the idea of intellectual development,
natural and obvious as this form of organization has come
to seem since Vico's day. Some people might be tempted to
take this fact as one more piece of evidence in favour of the
proposition that Vico was ahead of his time. However, the
idea of writing the autobiography was not his own. The
work was actually commissioned by a certain Count
Porcía, a soldier of literary inclinations who was in the
service of the Republic of Venice, and it was part of a general
project for collecting the intellectual autobiographies of
distinguished men in order to document their methods of
study and the obstacles which they had found in their way
so as to be able to reform the educational system and place
it on a sound empirical basis. The project was probably the
idea of the Venetian polymath, the friar and architect Carlo
Lodoli (1690–1761), an admirer of Vico and, like him, a
gifted man who was not fully appreciated in his own day.

Like his other works, Vico's autobiography is sometimes
unreliable on matters of fact. It provides no more reliable
an account of his early life than can reasonably be expected
from the memory of a man in his later fifties, and it is not
altogether consistent with Vico's surviving letters or with
the testimony of his contemporaries. However, this source
does have the very great advantage of allowing us to see Vico
from within and also of giving us an impression of the
intellectual stages through which he passed.

Vico was born in Naples, the son of a bookseller. Born in 1668, he was over thirty when the eighteenth century began, and by the 1720s he had come to believe that he was living in an age of decline. For these reasons he may be regarded as an essentially seventeenth-century figure. As a child, he tells us, he fractured his skull in a fall, and he grew up 'melancholy', as he puts it, in poor health, with a bent for solitary study which was doubtless encouraged by his living in a bookshop. The education he received from a series of Neapolitan clergymen was something of a recapitulation of the intellectual trends of the previous four hundred years or so, from the scholastic philosophers to the baroque rhetoricians. Alone or with his teachers, Vico studied the well-known logic textbook of Peter of Spain (1226–76), the philosophy of the British Franciscan Duns Scotus (1265–1308), and the metaphysics of the Spanish Jesuit Francisco Suarez (1548–1617), who integrated some Renaissance ideas into the medieval philosophical tradition. Vico tells us in his vivid way that he 'shut himself up in his house for a year to study Suarez'. He learned, in short, to be a Christian Aristotelian.

Vico also underwent the classical education which had become the norm since the Renaissance, and learned to write both Latin prose and Latin verse. At about the age of seventeen he was encouraged by his father to apply himself to the indispensable study for ambitious young men of parts at that time—in other words, the law, or more exactly the 'two laws', civil law and canon law, the law of the state and that of the Church, both based to a large extent on Roman precedents. Vico's contemporary Giannone, who also grew up in Naples, underwent a similar course of study, from Duns Scotus to canon law, before becoming one of the major anti-clericals (as well as one of the major historians) of his age: the curriculum seems to have been fairly typical of the place and time. As a relaxation from these studies

Vico wrote poetry, at first in what he was to call 'the most corrupt modern manner' (in other words, the baroque), but later in a simpler, more classical style. He continued to be in demand for most of his life as a poet who could produce appropriate occasional verse, in Latin or Italian, to commemorate the weddings and the funerals of the Neapolitan aristocracy.

Vico studied his law at the University of Naples, and continued to read philosophy in his spare time, much of it spent in the countryside at Vatolla, near Salerno, where he was employed as private tutor to the sons of the local marquis.

The autobiography gives the impression that Vico was working out his ideas almost entirely by himself. However, other sources suggest that at this time, when he was in his early twenties, he was part of a group of men of letters in Naples. Italian intellectuals of the period liked to meet in more or less formal clubs, academies, and salons to listen to papers on a wide variety of subjects and then to discuss them. Despite his self-image of the solitary thinker, so memorably delineated in the autobiography, Vico was not unclubbable. He discovered a number of congenial spirits among his contemporaries. Indeed, he admits to having written more than one of his books in the evening in the midst of conversations with his friends. He frequented several academies and salons and so participated fully in the intellectual life of the city.

In the late seventeenth century, this city was no backwater. Naples was a metropolis, one of the largest cities in Europe, with a population of about half a million, which was less than that of London or Paris at this time but considerably more than that of (say) Amsterdam, despite the general prosperity of the Dutch Republic. Naples was not such a great centre of intellectual innovation as Paris, London, and Amsterdam all were in this period, but all the same it was the scene of some lively debates. It was, indeed, becoming the arena for a major confrontation between the rival supporters of tradition and innovation, intellectual orthodoxy and intellectual heterodoxy, ancients and moderns.

In the later seventeenth century, a small group of outward-looking Neapolitan intellectuals, for the most part either lawyers or physicians, were coming to reject the authority of the ancients, such as Hippocrates (*c*.460–*c*.380 BC) and Galen (*c*.129–99 BC) in medicine, and Aristotle (384–322 BC) in a wide range of subjects (Aristotle was still *the* authority in the eyes of most seventeenth-century European intellectuals, a position he had held since his rediscovery in the thirteenth century). These Neapolitans—notably Tommaso Cornelio (1614–84), who was professor of medicine and mathematics at the university, Leonardo di Capoa (1617–95), a physician, and Francesco D'Andrea (1625–98), a leading lawyer—were all enthusiasts for the 'new philosophy', as it was called at the time: in other words for the ideas of Galileo, Bacon, and Descartes, ideas which they frequently discussed in their academy of the 'Investigators'.

These 'moderns' did not reject the study of classical antiquity altogether. What they did was to support what might be called an 'alternative antiquity' which was not Aristotelian, perhaps to camouflage the novelty of their views and to widen their appeal by giving them a pedigree or perhaps because they were genuinely impressed by some ancient ideas. They were, for example, interested in Plato and also in the neoplatonic tradition of Renaissance Italy, a tradition into which they assimilated Descartes. Like a number of French and English intellectuals of the period, the Neapolitan group was also interested in the Greek philosopher Epicurus (341–270 BC) and his follower the Roman poet Lucretius (*c*.95–55 BC).

The appeal of the ideas of Epicurus and Lucretius was that they offered a means of liberation from the 'tyranny of Aristotle', as Leonardo di Capoa put it. However, the ideas of the Epicureans undermined not only Aristotle and the medieval scholastic philosophers who accepted his authority, but Christianity as well. After all, Epicurus had taught that the origin of religion was fear and that the universe was not created by design but was merely the product of a chance combination of atoms. Yet it would be misleading to give the impression that this Neapolitan group was a circle of atheists. Like the French philosopher Pierre Gassendi (1592–1655), whose work they knew and admired, the Investigators seem to have tried to reconcile the ideas of Epicurus with those of Catholicism. Nevertheless, it is scarcely surprising to discover that the Inquisition of Naples took a rather different view of their activities.

In the Protestant world at this time, the supporters of the new philosophy included a number of clergymen and even a few bishops, such as Wilkins of Chester, who wrote on mathematics; Sprat of Rochester, who wrote a history of the Royal Society; and Burnet of Salisbury. The same was true, if to a lesser extent, in Catholic France. Gassendi was a priest and Marin Mersenne, another leading figure in the scientific revolution, was a friar. In Italy, however, as in Spain, the clergy were generally hostile to the new ideas, more especially after the Galileo affair (Galileo had been condemned in 1633). An English visitor to Naples in 1664, who attended a meeting of the Investigators, recorded the complaint of the intellectuals he met 'of the Inquisition, and their clergymen's opposition to the new philosophy; and of the difficulty they met with in getting books out of England, Holland etc'. It was necessary to get special permission to read works which were on the Church's Index of Prohibited Books, and this permission was not always forthcoming. In 1685, another British visitor to

Naples and the Investigators, the bishop Gilbert Burnet, noted that there were 'societies of men at Naples of freer thoughts than can be found in any other place of Italy', adding that they were 'ill looked on by the clergy and represented as a set of atheists'. There was a dramatic confirmation of the truth of Burnet's observation six years later, in 1691, when a trial took place at Naples of four men accused by the Inquisition of believing that the universe was composed of atoms; that there were men on earth before Adam (so that the Bible gave only a partial account of the origins of mankind); and that Christ was an impostor. Two of the accused were friends of Vico, who was twenty-three years old at the time of the trial.

The dangers of unorthodoxy in early modern Italy must not be forgotten, and the possibility has to be borne in mind when reading Vico that he harboured more unorthodox ideas than he was prepared to admit openly (below, pp. 85–6). However, it is also important to remember that the Inquisition was quite unable to stifle the Neapolitan debate between ancients and moderns. In the course of this debate Vico's ideas took form. They were in a number of cases a synthesis of opposing positions, or an attempt to go beyond them.

As was the 'fashion'—his own term—in Naples in his day, Vico was interested in the ideas of Epicurus and Gassendi. Indeed, he seems to have passed through an Epicurean phase, which is not mentioned in the autobiography, perhaps for reasons of prudence, but left traces on a poem, *Emotions of Despair* (*Affetti di un Disperato*), which he published when he was twenty-five. The pessimism of this lament—in which the poet describes himself as 'at war' against himself and his age as an 'iron age' which 'draws to its fall'—has suggested to more than one student of Vico that he must have gone through some sort of spiritual crisis at this time. In later life he explicitly and

15

strongly rejected the Epicurean belief in chance, but the famous image of primitive society presented in the *New Science*, an image of men and women living in the forest like wild animals, remains close to that of Lucretius in his great philosophical poem *On the Nature of the Universe*, down to the clap of thunder which makes them believe in a god.

It was probably at this stage in his career that Vico discovered the *Politico-Theological Treatise* of a thinker whom some of his contemporaries described as 'Epicurean', the Dutch-Jewish philosopher Baruch Spinoza (1632–77). In later life, Vico was to refer to Spinoza only to refute him, but the *Treatise*, which deals among other subjects, with the poetry of the Bible, probably made a greater impression on him than he was ever prepared to admit.

Like many of his contemporaries, Vico also went through a phase of enthusiasm for the ideas of René Descartes (1596–1650), in 'science' (as we would call it) as well as in pure 'philosophy'. According to his autobiography, Vico 'heard that the physics of René Descartes had eclipsed all preceding systems, so that he was inflamed with a desire to have knowledge of it' (A 128). Vico seems to have read Descartes in Latin, and it was probably in a Latin translation that he became acquainted with *The Search for Truth* by Descartes's follower the French priest Nicolas Malebranche (1638–1715), a treatise which discusses the senses, the imagination, and the passions as obstacles to the attainment of the truth and offers a method, modelled on that of mathematics, by which these obstacles may be avoided. In later life Vico became disenchanted with the ideas of Descartes, but he did not lose his admiration for his geometrical method. Indeed, he was to present the major conclusions of his *New Science* in the geometrical form of deductions from a set of axioms. Vico's autobiography also follows Descartes: it is modelled on Descartes's account, in his *Discourse on Method*, of his intellectual development. It is true that he accused Descartes of giving a false account of his life in order to make his philosophy seem more impressive, but all the same, Vico's attempt to demonstrate that 'his intellectual life was bound to have been such as it was and not otherwise' (A 182) is a Cartesian one.

In 1699, Vico was appointed professor of rhetoric at the University of Naples, a post he was to hold for more than forty years. The duties included delivering an annual oration to inaugurate the academic year. Vico's surviving orations for the period 1699–1706 deal with education and its proper functions and methods. Concerned as they are with such traditional themes as the compatibility of arms and letters, these orations might easily be mistaken for the work of a Renaissance humanist, were it not for their references to the natural sciences, and their critique of the antiquarian and philological traditions. Descartes had made fun of antiquarians whose main object in life was to discover information about ancient Rome which Cicero's servant-girl (say) had known without research, and Vico wrote in similar vein, in his third oration (1701):

> You boast, philologist, of your complete knowledge of Roman furniture and costume, and of knowing the streets and quarters of Rome better than those of your own city. What are you so proud of? All you know is what was familiar to a Roman potter, cook, shoemaker, traveller, or town crier.

This critique should not, however, be taken to imply that Vico rejected the study of the classical past in any form. In the same year in which he obtained his professorship, he became a member of the Palatine Academy, a group which had taken the place of the Investigators as the leading learned society of Naples, and which enjoyed the patronage and protection of the King of Spain's viceroy in Naples. Its members included the literary critic Gregorio Caloprese (1650–1715) and his pupil the philosopher Paolo Mattia Doria (1662–1746), who were both admirers of Plato and Descartes, as Vico was at the time; and also Giuseppe Valletta (1636–1714), a lawyer of wide interests who defended the philosophy of Descartes against the Inquisition, built up a large and famous library in which Vico was able to work, and encouraged him to publish his poem *Emotions of Despair*.

The Palatine Academy was much concerned with the study of antiquity. At its meetings the members read papers on such topics as the philosophy of the ancient Assyrians and the policies of various Roman emperors, including Claudius and Caligula. Vico's own contribution to the proceedings was a paper *On the Sumptuous Feasts of the Romans*. It was not, however, an essay in pure antiquarianism, which merely provided information which would have been familiar to a Roman cook; it was a story with a moral, arguing that conquering Rome had itself been conquered by Asian luxury. The other topics debated by the academicians were not necessarily as irrelevant to the contemporary world as they may now seem, since analogies were often drawn between ancient and modern philosophies, and between the decline of Rome and that of the Spanish empire, of which Naples was still a part.

At the beginnning of the new century, then, the thirty-two-year-old Vico had settled into academic life, and he had already displayed a range of interests which were unusually wide even in that relatively unspecialized age. A teacher of rhetoric, he was also a student of the law and a philosopher aware of recent development in mathematics and the physical sciences (magnetism and medicine were among the subjects which he used to discuss with his friend Doria). He was a practising poet, associated with another academy, that of Arcadia, which stood for the purification of poetry from the excesses of the style now known as 'baroque'; the style he favoured was austere rather than grand or playful, aiming at sublimity rather than magnificence or astonishment. As for history, Vico's essay on the decline of the Roman empire was soon followed by another short work, an account of an unsuccessful conspiracy against the Spanish regime which was planned at Naples in 1701. Composed about two years later, the *Conspiracy of the Princes of Naples* remained unpublished in Vico's lifetime. Written in classical Latin, following the obvious model of the *Conspiracy of Catiline* by the Roman historian Sallust (86–*c*.34 BC), with formal character-sketches of the protagonists and an oration put into the mouth of the viceroy, this account contrives to integrate into its fast-moving narrative such economic details as the run on the banks and observations on the trade between Spain and England. An ancient Roman would have considered such details beneath the dignity of history, but they were now coming to be taken rather more seriously.

With these achievements to his credit, Vico still had a long way to go in his intellectual development. Looking back from the 1720s at the itinerary he had followed, he identified four milestones along the route, four authors to whom he was particularly indebted. Two of these authors were ancient, and two modern. They were Plato, Tacitus, Bacon, and Grotius.

Of these four, the first two already formed part of Vico's culture by 1700. The appeal of Plato—together with his Renaissance followers—was manifold. Vico was, for instance, attracted by Plato's theories of language (below, pp. 39–41). He also admired the 'divine Plato', as he sometimes called him, because he portrayed man 'as he should be', in his descriptions of the ideal society in the *Republic* and the *Laws*. By the time that Vico came to write the *New*

Science, he had moved some distance away from Plato. All the same, there is something reminiscent of Plato's doctrine of ideas in the discussion, central to Vico's book, of what he called an 'ideal eternal history' in the sense of a stable pattern underlying the apparent flux of events. He was interested not only in Plato but also in the Neoplatonists of late antiquity, such as Iamblichus, and of the Renaissance—Ficino, Pico, and other students of the 'hermetic tradition', in other words the ancient wisdom attributed to the Egyptian sage Hermes Trismegistus.

Just as Vico's 'Plato' includes the neoplatonists, so his 'Tacitus' extends to the so-called 'Tacitists' of the seventeenth century. For Cornelius Tacitus (born *c*. AD 55), the great historian of Imperial Rome, was the object of particular admiration in the seventeenth century, when commentators saw many analogies between the Roman emperors and the absolute monarchs of their own day, and attempted to construct a system out of his many incidental pessimistic remarks on the nature of man and politics. They tended to assimilate the views of Tacitus to those of Niccolo Machiavelli (1469–1527), a political theorist with an equally low view of human nature but rather more interest in systematization. Like Spinoza, Machiavelli was a thinker in whom Vico took more interest than he cared to admit.

A similar concern with both Plato and Tacitus was shown by a number of the lecturers on the Roman empire at the Palatine Academy. They doubtless helped Vico, who was more of a philosopher than Tacitus and more of a historian than Plato, to make a synthesis of his two ancient authors, the one who 'contemplates man as he is', and the one who considered him 'as he should be'. To link the ideal with the real was in fact the great enterprise of Vico's intellectual life.

As for his two modern authors, Bacon and Grotius, Vico

discovered them only when he had reached early middle age. They were both Protestant northerners of the early seventeenth century.

Francis Bacon (1561–1626), the arch-empiricist, does not exactly seem an obvious choice of model for an ardent Platonist and Cartesian, as Vico still was at the time of his discovery, about 1707. What first attracted him to Bacon was a little Latin treatise *On the Wisdom of the Ancients*, which interpreted the classical myths as political or scientific allegories, concerned with a prince's need for a favourite (symbolized by Endymion), for example, or with the atomic structure of the universe (symbolized, improbable as this sounds, by Cupid). Vico would later describe this treatise as 'more ingenious and learned than true', but at the time of his discovery he seems to have found it convincing. Still more appealing to him was Bacon's *Advancement of Learning*—or more exactly, its Latin version, *De Augmentis Scientiarum*, for Vico is unlikely to have been able to read English. In this book he could find a survey of the different departments of knowledge, an analysis of the current defects in each, and recommendations for reform. Also relevant to Vico's concerns at this time was Bacon's *Novum Organum*, which consists largely of aphorisms laying down the rules to be followed in the investigation of the natural world.

Vico's account of his four authors has sometimes been interpreted as a kind of allegory of his intellectual development, a sort of private myth. Whether this was the case or not, it is abundantly clear that he was no mere passive recipient of 'influence'. Ideas attracted into his magnetic field were necessarily changed as they were incorporated into a system with numerous and strong relationships between its constituent parts. He sometimes projected his own attitudes onto the authors he studied: Tacitus, for example, he saw as a metaphysician. What he took from his authors he transformed, assimilated, made his own. A fair example of such assimilation is his inaugural oration of 1708, *On the Study Methods of Our Time*.

The oration begins with a reference to the *Advancement of Learning*, and it ranges over the arts and sciences in the same ambitious way Bacon had done. It is essentially concerned with the question whether the intellectual achievements of the ancients are greater than those of the moderns, or vice versa. Vico does not come down on either side; he prefers to draw distinctions. He praises the achievements of the 'new critical method' (in other words, the geometrical method of Descartes and his followers), particularly in mathematics. However, despite the claim that it is 'common to all the sciences and arts', Vico denies the applicability of this method to the field of practical wisdom, to ethics, politics, and law. In this field, Vico concluded, the methods of the ancients remain superior, and he criticizes the Cartesians for distracting attention from the world of man. In other words, Vico had not been converted to Baconian empiricism, but the encounter with Bacon's thought had liberated him from Descartes and left him critical of the critical method. Where Descartes had emphasized the need for 'clear and distinct ideas', Vico asserted that apparently clear and distinct knowledge was a vice, not a virtue of the human understanding.

What he wanted to put in its place begins to emerge, if somewhat obscurely, from his first major work, published in 1710, *On the Ancient Wisdom of the Italians*. The book, which is written in Latin, is dedicated to Vico's friend Paolo Mattia Doria and presented as the continuation of a discussion begun after dinner at Doria's house. It is offered as a modest contribution towards the achievement of Bacon's ideal of the advancement of learning, but it is modelled on Plato's *Cratylus*, a discussion of etymology which Vico interprets as Plato's attempt to discover the 'ancient wisdom of the Greeks'.

Vico observes that 'the origins of a great number of words were so scholarly that they seem to have arisen not from common popular usage but from some inner learning'. Since the early Romans 'had no pursuits other than agriculture and war', he concluded that these terms had been 'taken over from some other learned race', such as the Etruscans (W 49). What he attempted was to reconstruct the beliefs of the early philosophers of Italy on the basis of the etymology of certain Latin words. For example, he related the word *fatum*, 'fate', to *factum*, 'made', and also to *fatus est*, 'he spoke', arguing that the Italian philosophers must have thought that fate was inexorable because 'created things are God's words', and 'what is made cannot be unmade'. Again, he pointed out that whereas moderns claim to think with their brains, the ancient Romans believed that they thought with their hearts.

Having reconstructed this ancient philosophy, Vico went on to employ it as a weapon against the geometrical method and the clear and distinct ideas of the Cartesians, emphasizing instead the practical wisdom of which he had spoken in the 1708 oration and also what he called *ingenium*, defined as 'the power of connecting separate and diverse elements'. Vico the poet was beginning to assist Vico the philosopher.

The reaction of contemporaries to *On the Ancient Wisdom of the Italians* was not unlike their later reception of the *New Science*. The book was discussed in one of the reviews which were beginning to be founded at this time, the Venetian 'Literary Journal' (*Giornale de'Letterati*), and it was judged to be both too obscure and too speculative. Vico was offended by these criticisms, and he wrote two long letters to the journal insisting that he had proved his

23

points. Not for the last time in his intellectual career, he felt himself to have been misunderstood.

It was perhaps for this reason that he left his *Ancient Wisdom* unfinished, lacking the sections he had planned on logic, physics, and ethics. Instead of carrying on with his philosophical etymology, he turned to biography. At the suggestion of one of his pupils, who was a nephew of the great man, Vico wrote a life of the Neapolitan aristocrat Antonio Caraffa (1642–93), who had been the commander of the imperial forces in Hungary at the time of Count Tököly's rebellion against the emperor Leopold I. The biography, written in Latin, belongs, like the account of the 1701 conspiracy, to the tradition of humanist historiography. It contains speeches attributed to the hero and other literary set-pieces such as the description of the Turkish siege of Vienna of 1683. It follows classical models, notably Tacitus, and describes military operations in terms of legions and centurions. However, such Turkish terms as 'vizier', 'janissaries' (infantry), and 'spahis' (cavalry) also occur in Vico's pages, despite the otherwise classical Latin. These terms had to occur because Vico's aim was to write a history of the kind which Bacon had recommended, a history which would 'make men wise', and because he believed that the particular value of history was to enable the reader to understand 'the small things which have great consequences'. The local details are therefore important, and Vico's biography of the minor Neapolitan general is not so remote from its author's philosophical interests as it may look.

The *Life of Antonio Caraffa* is important in Vico's development for another reason as well. This biography of a local aristocrat, based on the family papers, encouraged Vico to widen his horizons and to concern himself not only with the policies of Louis XIV, which he had already discussed in his *Conspiracy of the Princes of Naples*, but

with Hungary and the Ottoman Empire as well. To eval-
uate Caraffa—whose repressive regime is remembered by
Hungarians to this day—Vico found himself 'obliged', as he
put it, to return to his legal studies, and in particular to read
the treatise on the *Law of War and Peace* by the great Dutch
scholar Hugo de Groot, better known as Grotius
(1583–1645). A number of Vico's friends such as Valletta
and Doria, were interested in the ideas of Grotius. As for
Vico himself, the *Law of War and Peace*, which he read in
his mid-forties, impressed him so much that he wrote a
commentary on it (now lost), and came to regard Grotius
as his 'fourth author', on a par with Plato, Tacitus, and
Bacon. What appealed to him in the work of Grotius was
that he 'embraces in a system of universal law the whole of
philosophy and philology' (A 155), thus revealing the
relationship between social practice and its principles and
providing a non-Cartesian system of the sciences of man
(see below, p. 78). On the other hand, Vico criticized
Grotius because he gave no place in his system to
providence. At once excited and dissatisfied by Grotius, he
abandoned his commentary and began to consider a treatise
of his own on the subject of jurisprudence. This treatise,
which has come to be known as the *Universal Law*, was
published in three parts between 1720 and 1722.

According to Vico, the philosophical foundations of law
are first, man's natural equity and sociability, and second,
but no less important, divine providence. He thus parts
company with Grotius on the question of providence, but
he appeals to Grotius against the view that men join
together and form societies merely out of self-interest, a
view which Vico associates with 'sceptics', as he calls
them, such as Machiavelli and Hobbes. As for the historical
origins of law, in his search for them Vico goes back to the
time when men and women wandered the earth like wild
beasts, and he describes the rise of different forms of society

in chronological order—families, retinues, aristocracies, monarchies, and democracies, each with its own form of law, whether public or private, severe or 'benign'. Vico proceeds to relate this political history of mankind to the psychological development of the human race, from its 'childhood', when reason was weak and imagination strong, to maturity and rationality. He also discusses the history of language, literature, and religion; the meaning of the Greek myths; the origins of Italian culture; and many other topics, some of them to all appearances quite remote from jurisprudence. If the point of these discussions is to suggest that variations in law cannot be understood without looking at variations in the rest of culture, it is a point which never becomes explicit.

The *Universal Law* had a mixed reception. Some contemporaries complained of its obscurity, while others, including Jean Le Clerc (1657–1736), the editor of one of the leading reviews of the day, the *Bibliothèque Universelle*, found much to admire in it. Vico himself had enough confidence in his contribution to jurisprudence to compete, in 1723, for the vacant chair of civil law at the University of Naples. He gave a trial lecture, as was the custom, but he was rejected. Disillusioned with the law, he used his leisure to develop a still more ambitious project. To his rejection by the lawyers we doubtless owe his most important work, the one for which he is remembered today, the *New Science*, first published in 1725, when he was fifty-seven. Unlike his earlier books it was written not in Latin but in Italian, as if intended for a non-academic audience.

The *Principles of a New Science concerning the Common Nature of Nations*, as Vico called it, was in fact not so much a change of direction as a widening and a deepening of some major themes in the *Universal Law*, which even includes a chapter with the title 'a New Science is attempted'. It also refers back to the *Ancient Wisdom of the Italians.* Vico's wide interests were at last coming to focus on one central problem. He was still concerned with establishing the principles of natural law, and it was for this purpose that he attempted his conjectural reconstruction of the world of primitive man ('the first men' is his usual phrase). He was still in search of ancient wisdom, but he no longer believed that this wisdom was the achievement of the early philosophers. On the contrary, it was really 'popular wisdom' (*sapienza volgare*), expressing itself through traditions, myths, and rituals. Vico was by now convinced that his predecessors, including Plato and Bacon as well as Machiavelli and Grotius, had been guilty of an enormous anachronism. They had imagined early men 'in accordance with our present ideas and not in accordance with the original ideas proper to them'. What was necessary was, 'by a supreme effort', to divest the mind of modern assumptions and 'enter, through the force of our understanding, the nature of the first men' (N1. 77–80).

Vico thus found himself obliged to investigate the history of thought as well as the history of institutions, and to relate the two even more closely than he had tried to do in the *Universal Law.* He distinguished three periods, or, to use the late classical phrase he made his own, 'three sects of times' (*tre sette de'tempi*). These three periods were the 'superstitious', the 'heroic', and the 'human', each with its own form of law and its own view of the world. Each period also developed its own kind of language, for the 'basic principle of this science', discovered, so Vico claimed, after twenty-five years' meditation, was that the first men were poets, imaginative rather than rational, and thinking in a concrete manner rather than an abstract one, as their rituals, symbols, and myths revealed. The poet and the professor of rhetoric had come to the assistance of the ancient historian and the philosopher of law.

Vico had great hopes for his *New Science*, and he seems

to have thought that it would do for the study of society (the 'civil world' or 'world of nations' as he calls it), what had recently been done for the world of nature by the *Principia Mathematica* of the great scientist Sir Isaac Newton (1642–1727). At all events, he sent a copy of his treatise to Sir Isaac via a rabbi of Livorno (Leghorn). It is not known whether this presentation copy ever reached its destination. Another copy went by the same route to Le Clerc, who had expressed admiration for the *Universal Law*, but Vico's gift did not elicit a response in this case either. The author was bitterly disappointed with the public reaction to his book, or to be more exact, with the lack of reaction. 'In this city', he wrote from Naples, 'I reckon that I have sent it to the desert, and I avoid all the main centres so as not to meet the people to whom I have sent copies, and if I cannot avoid them, I greet them hastily; and when this happens none of them give any sign of having read it, and so confirm me in my opinion that I have sent it to the desert.' Since the ideas of Descartes remained so fashionable in Naples, Vico commented sadly in another of his letters, it was only to be expected that his own work would be condemned.

Vico's disappointment was somewhat mitigated when he learned that there were laudatory letters waiting for him at the post office. These letters included one from Carlo Lodoli, in Venice, informing him of the enthusiasm for his book among the 'men of distinction' there, and suggesting an immediate reprint. With a somewhat pathetic need for reassurance, Vico reproduced the whole letter in his autobiography, itself written, as we have seen, at Lodoli's indirect suggestion.

On the other hand, the review of the *New Science* in the *Acta Eruditorum* ('Proceedings of Scholars') of Leipzig, a journal with a wide international circulation, was an unfavourable one. Indeed, Vico considered it a 'gross misrepresentation' and felt obliged to reply to it at length, as he had once answered the criticisms of his *Ancient Wisdom of the Italians*. His sense of being misunderstood and unrecognized, 'a foreigner in his own country', was only confirmed. Indeed, in the 1720s, if not before, Vico seems to have withdrawn from society and retired 'to his desk, as to his high impregnable citadel' (A 200). In his melancholy solitude he appears even to have given up reading, or at least to have given up reading newly published books. To one of his foreign correspondents he wrote that in Naples the republic of letters was 'near its end', for books in Greek and Latin were falling in price for lack of demand. He knew this well because he had made the valuation of the magnificent collection of his old friend and patron, the late Giuseppe Valletta, who had died in 1714. This criterion of the health of a culture suggests that at heart Vico was a humanist. He was becoming increasingly remote from the new intellectual trends of his time, as he realized himself, writing in his autobiography that the reason that fortune is said to favour the young is that 'as the world by its nature changes in taste from year to year, they later find themselves in their old age strong in such wisdom as no longer pleases and therefore no longer profits' (A 137). He was at least able to see his own case in historical perspective.

Vico continued to deliver special orations, notably one 'On the Heroic Mind' (1732), praising the achievements of Columbus and—despite all his criticisms—Descartes. He revised his rhetoric textbook for a second edition. He went on composing occasional verses for the Neapolitan aristocracy. In 1735, at the age of sixty-seven, he was appointed official historian to the new ruler of Naples, Charles Bourbon.

However, his main concern was to continue meditating on his *New Science*. There were so many stages of revision that the final version is sometimes called the ninth, but there were only three editions. The first edition had come out in 1725. The second, published in 1730, was a major reorganization of the material. The third edition, revised and enlarged, appeared in 1744, just after the author's death. In this final version, the *New Science* was divided into five books. There was an elaborate allegorical frontispiece, designed by a local artist, Domenico Vaccaro, with the author's assistance, followed by an introduction explaining the iconography and by this indirect means giving the reader a preliminary 'Idea of the Work'. There was a chronological table, as there had been in the *Universal Law*, but much more extensive. Its seven columns placed in parallel the major events in the histories of seven peoples: the Hebrews, Chaldeans, Scythians (who have only one entry), Phoenicians, Egyptians, Greeks, and Romans.

Book One was now devoted to the 'establishment of principles', and it included one hundred and fourteen 'dignities', as Vico called them, or axioms, which summarized the main assumptions and conclusions of the whole work. Book Two, 'Poetic Wisdom', was concerned with what was called the 'master key of this science', the comparison between children, poets, and primitive men, developing the comparison at length and describing 'poetic logic', 'poetic politics', 'poetic chronology', 'poetic geography', and so on. Book Three, 'The Discovery of the True Homer', expressed a radical change of mind on Vico's part. He had long been using the Homeric poems as a source, or, as he liked to put it, a 'treasury' of ancient customs; but by now he had reached the conclusion that these poems had been elaborated over a long period and that the individual we call 'Homer' was not fact but fiction. Book Four, 'The Course the Nations Run', developed more fully the idea of the sequence, or *corso*, of three ages in human history ('divine', 'heroic', and 'human', as he called them in his vivid way), each with its own kind of custom, law, language, government, and even its own type of human nature. The sequence was not irreversible according to Vico, and Book Five, taking up and developing an idea expressed rather briefly in the first edition, dealt with the *ricorso*, the return or 're-run' of an earlier age. The European Middle Ages, for example, were presented as a second age of heroes or barbarians.

The book as a whole is still presented as a 'system of natural law', but its other aspects, of which Vico now distinguished no fewer than six, were now given rather more emphasis. It was, he pointed out, a 'history of human ideas', for changes in ideas underlay changes in customs. It was a 'historical mythology' because it offered a new approach to the interpretation of myth, and it was a 'new art of criticism' because it laid down rules for discerning the true elements in otherwise fabulous histories. It was also a 'civil theology' because it revealed the workings of providence among the gentiles. 'Out of the passions of men each bent on his private advantage . . . it has made the civil institutions (*ordini civili*), by which they may live in human society' (N2. 133).

The 1744 version of the *New Science* was also revised by the author according to literary criteria. The new text was harder to follow than before, written as it was in a still more personal style which was turning into a private language as its author withdrew further into himself. The revised version is also more vivid, more concrete, more poetic, or—to use a favourite term of Vico's—more 'sublime'.

It is this final version, the third edition (confusingly known as the 'second *New Science*'), which is discussed at greater length in the next chapter.

3 The *New Science*

The *New Science* is a book stuffed so full of ideas that it almost bursts at the seams. It is at once a study of history, philosophy, poetry, theology, and law, and it also deals with problems which have since become central to such disciplines as sociology and social anthropology. It is no wonder that Vico found difficulty in ordering his material, as the many changes he made in the book's arrangement would suggest. As for his modern readers, they often find this arrangement hard to follow. For this reason it seems better not to discuss the text section by section, but instead to select and comment upon a small number of major themes, four in particular. They are law, language and myth, the course of history, and lastly the sources, methods, and scientific status of the *New Science*. In all four of these themes an attempt will be made to compare and contrast Vico with his contemporaries and predecessors. In other words, his work will be replaced in its cultural context in order to determine to what extent and in what precise ways his thinking was original.

Law

Vico presented the *New Science* as a 'system of natural law'. The idea of natural law is an old one, going back at least as far as Aristotle. In his *Ethics*, Aristotle rejected the view that justice is a matter of mere convention and differs from one place to another. What he did was to draw a sharp distinction between justice and customs. Customs were rules established by convention on the grounds of convenience—weights and measures, for example—and they did indeed vary from place to place. Justice, on the other hand, was considered by Aristotle to be 'natural', unchanging, and universal. A similar distinction was made by the ancient Roman writers on law, who equated the law of nature with the conclusions of what they called 'right reason'; and also by medieval philosophers, notably Thomas Aquinas (*c.*1225–74), whose achievement was to make a synthesis of the ideas of Aristotle with Western Christian tradition of the thirteenth century.

In the sixteenth and seventeenth centuries, the concept of natural law became the focus of a lively and protracted debate. The controversy was stimulated by the discovery of America, a new world which seemed strange to Europeans and so raised once more the old question whether any order underlay the apparent diversity of human customs. The debate was also encouraged by the rise of centralized nation-states. If each nation had the right to make its own rules or 'positive laws', it was far from clear what rules should govern the relations between states. Was the law of nations the law of nature? Was this the law followed in the days before organized societies or states had come into existence? These are among the questions discussed in the seventeenth century by the Spanish philosopher Suarez (whom Vico studied in his youth, as we have seen), as well as by the three 'princes' of natural law, as Vico liked to call them, Grotius, Selden, and Pufendorf.

In his *Law of War and Peace* (1625), Grotius set out to write a treatise on international law. He therefore needed to discuss the law of nature. He defined it as the dictates of 'right reason' or 'common sense', summarized it as respect for the rights of others, equated it, as others had done before him, with the law of nations, and declared that it would retain its validity even if God did not exist. He accepted Aristotle's description of man as a gentle, sociable animal. The Englishman John Selden (1584–1654), a scholar of wide interests, compared the customs of the Hebrews with the principles of natural law, which he defined as 'what natural reason establishes for all men'. Selden held the unusual view that early men had lived in a state of complete moral freedom until they came to know God's commands. As for the German jurist Samuel Pufendorf (1632–94), he reiterated the more common Aristotelian view that early man was ruled by the laws of nature, of which the most fundamental is the law of sociability. Living in society is living according to human nature. Like that of Grotius, Pufendorf's system of natural law does not require God to make it work.

As for Vico, he was pulled in two opposite directions. He was close enough to Plato—and to Suarez—to believe in a universal eternal justice. Indeed, he reproached his 'princes' with giving too secular an account of natural law, which Vico considered to be the work of divine providence. He criticized Pufendorf for his 'Epicurean hypothesis, supposing man to have been cast into the world without any help or care from God' (N2. 397).

On the other hand, Vico's acute sense of change and anachronism gave him some sympathy for the relativist position of the 'sceptics', as he called them. He was particularly unhappy with the conventional natural-law account of the life of early man in the so-called 'state of nature', before the rise of civil society,

> For the philosophers have meditated upon a human nature already civilised by the religions and laws in which, and only in which, philosophers originated, and not upon the human nature which gave rise to the religions and laws in which philosophers originated. (N2. 23)

Pufendorf had derived his picture of early man in the state of nature by taking man 'as he now is' and imagining society as non-existent. Vico objected that this was starting in the middle instead of going back to the beginning. In a similar way to Vico (whose work he does not seem to have known), Jean-Jacques Rousseau (1712–78) was to criticize John Locke's picture of primitive man for being no more than an image of modern man in a primitive environment, while David Hume (1711–76) also argued that early men, in their 'wild uncultivated state', could not have realized the advantages of the social contract, as Locke and Pufendorf assumed.

Vico's own view of the state of nature was very different. According to him, it was a time when men were 'insensate and horrible beasts' (*bestioni*), with slow minds in giant bodies. This is a view not far removed in some respects from that of the English philosopher Thomas Hobbes (1588–1679), who described the state of nature quite unforgettably, in his treatise *Leviathan*, as a time when human life was 'solitary, poor, nasty, brutish, and short' (Vico does not seem to have known *Leviathan*, but he had read Hobbes's earlier Latin treatise *On the Citizen*, which expresses similar views). However, Vico could not agree with the Hobbesian account of man's exit from the state of nature, by way of fear and the pursuit of rational self-interest. So his attempted solution of the problem of the nature of natural law took the form of a synthesis of opposed views. He argued that natural law was indeed 'eternal in its idea', but that it necessarily went through various stages and took different forms in different periods (his three ages), because human nature has itself developed by stages in the course of history.

In this way Vico was led to discuss differences in customs and in the laws current in different places and times, in order to show that these differences are quite natural, indeed necessary. He had most to say about Roman law, the 'civil law' as it was called in his day, which he had studied in his youth, together with many of his contemporaries, because it was still the law of the land in southern Italy as in many other parts of Europe. This Roman law had been handed down to the Middle Ages in the form given it, in the sixth century, by the Byzantine emperor Justinian and his minister Tribonian, and it had subsequently been interpreted, applied, and adapted to new circumstances (whether the adaptation was conscious or unconscious) by a long succession of jurists from the eleventh century onwards in the universities of Italy and France.

Vico's aim, however, like that of some of the humanist lawyers of the Renaissance, with whose work he was certainly familiar, was to strip away the layers of interpretation and to go back to the original Roman law underneath. Indeed, he tried to go right back to the origins of Roman law and to reconstruct the earliest Roman customs. That involved studying the 'Twelve Tables', or 'Twelve Tablets', a code of law which now survives only in fragments but which every schoolboy knew, or was supposed to know, by heart in classical times. These laws were believed to go back to the year 451 BC when, according to Roman tradition, a delegation had been sent to Greece to find out what laws had been established a century and a half earlier by the great Athenian reformer Solon. Vico, on the contrary, argued with characteristic vehemence in his *Universal Law*, and again in the *New Science*, that the Romans had not borrowed their laws from anyone. His own suggestion was that the Twelve Tables were a codification of local custom, the custom of the region of Latium, in which Rome is situated. At the same time, he regarded the code as a 'treasure house' of natural law because it showed what had been appropriate for that place, time, and form of human nature.

Even the Twelve Tables were not really primitive enough for Vico. He wanted to go back behind them to the time when such institutions as law-codes and cities did not yet exist. Before the 'benign jurisprudence' of Athens and

Rome, in other words the rule of law 'dictated by fully developed human reason', there was, according to Vico, an age when affairs were regulated by the 'right of private violence'. In the Homeric poems, which Vico put on a par with the Twelve Tables as a treasury of natural law, the Greeks can be seen to have had no law but that of force, which was 'the law of Achilles, who referred every right to the tip of his spear'. This was Vico's second, or 'heroic', age. Earlier still, in the first age, law was divine, 'for men believed themselves and all their institutions to depend on the gods' (N2. 922–4). Disputes were settled by appeals to divine judgement. Before this came the age of the Hobbesian—or Lucretian—state of nature, when men were not really men at all.

Vico's interest in order and dispute in the long period before the Twelve Tables marks him off from the humanist lawyers, just as his use of historical sources, such as the Homeric poems, distinguishes him from the speculations of the philosophers concerning the state of nature. His discussion of legal history offers a synthesis of opposites in yet another area, that of the origins of feudal law.

The humanist lawyers of the Renaissance had made the discovery that the medieval law of property, notably the tenure of land ('fiefs') on condition of knight-service, as it had developed in France, Italy, England, and elsewhere, was distinct from classical Roman law. Some of the humanists, such as the Frenchman Jacques Cujas (1522–90), argued that the origins of this law of fiefs, or 'feudal' law as it was called, were Roman, and that feudal 'vassals', holding land by virtue of performing military service for their lords, had developed out of ancient Roman 'clients', who had served their patrons in a similar manner, although the duties of clients were defined less precisely. Other scholars thought, on the contrary, that feudal law was the creation of the Gauls, or, as was suggested by another French scholar,

François Hotman (1524–90), that it was the work of those German barbarians who became known as the Franks.

This Renaissance debate was revived in late seventeenth-century Naples, where the power of the local 'barons' gave it some topicality. Vico himself was to quote the predilection for duels of the Neapolitan nobles of his own day as a survival of the custom of trial by combat characteristic of the heroic age; in other words, there was a place in his system for the phenomenon known by some modern sociologists as 'cultural lag'. The origin of fiefs was among the questions debated in the Palatine Academy in Vico's time, and another member of the Academy, Nicolo Caravita (1647–1717), who was one of Vico's patrons, held the chair of feudal law at the University of Naples. Cujas and Hotman, who appear in the *New Science* as 'Cuiacio' and 'Ottomano', were well known to the lawyers of Naples, and the question of the origin of fiefs was eagerly discussed. Vico's resolution of this controversial question was on the one hand to accept the analogy between vassals and clients urged by 'Romanists', such as Cujas, but on the other hand to reject, with 'Germanists' like Hotman, the derivation of one institution from the other. As in the case of the Twelve Tables and their presumed derivation from the laws of Solon, Vico denied that borrowing had taken place and emphasized instead autonomous internal development. The development followed parallel lines in ancient Rome and medieval Europe, so he suggested, simply because this military form of social organization was one aspect of the age of heroes, which has recurred more than once in human history. In short, the concept of legal evolution (as opposed to invention or diffusion) was important for Vico; consequently his book deserves an important place in any history of the idea of legal evolution.

Vico's concern with the relation of law to the society and culture which surround it is close to that of a younger man whose impact was much more immediate. Charles-Louis de Secondat, baron de Montesquieu (1689–1755), published his *Spirit of the Laws* in 1748. On his visit to Italy twenty years earlier, Montesquieu had actually been recommended to buy a copy of the *New Science*, published not long before. However, there is no evidence that he bought the book, let alone read it. Like Newton, Montesquieu seems not to have known how closely some of Vico's ideas resembled his own.

The startling originality of Vico's critique of diffusionism and of his positive alternative to it deserves emphasis. These were among the most fruitful ideas of this astonishingly fertile thinker. It may be—as the parallel with Montesquieu would suggest—that the time was in a sense 'ripe' for these innovations. But ideas, unlike fruit, do not ripen by themselves. They have to be thought through for the first time by individuals. Vico not only came out with these important ideas but also worked them out. His concept of internal development is one of his outstanding achievements.

Language and myth

Vico's reflections on the history of law were, as we have seen, much concerned with a problem raised by ancient Greek philosophers: did a law of nature exist, or were laws merely matters of convention? His ideas about the origin and history of language took off from a similar starting-point. The question whether language is natural or conventional is in fact the central theme of Plato's dialogue *Cratylus*. In this dialogue, the speaker Cratylus argues that the meanings of words have certain natural affinities with the things for which they stand, while Hermogenes counters with the assertion that words are quite arbitrary in origin and take their meaning purely from social convention. Socrates says—as usual—that he does not know which of them is right and proceeds, equally characteristically, both to produce and to undermine a series of etymologies which would link words closely to things.

In the sixteenth and seventeenth centuries, Plato's problem attracted much interest. The discovery of the New World, coupled with increasingly close contact with China and Japan, made Europeans more aware than they had been of the sheer variety of human languages, while the development of mathematics suggested to some intellectuals that it was possible to invent a 'universal language' in which there would be no room for misunderstanding because each sign would have only one meaning, while each meaning would be expressed by one sign. Gestures and images were cited as examples—if imperfect ones—of such universal languages, and they were also cited as examples of languages with natural rather than conventional meanings. Francis Bacon, in his *Advancement of Learning*, summed up Renaissance thought on the subject when he distinguished two kinds of language, the natural and the conventional, and included in his first category both the hieroglyphics of Egypt, which he, like his contemporaries, interpreted as symbolic images or 'emblems', and gestures, which he described as 'transitory hieroglyphics'.

In the linguistic debates of the sixteenth and seventeenth centuries, frequent reference was made not only to Plato but to the Bible as well. Scholars nourished the hope of getting back somehow behind the babble of Babel, of freeing mankind from the curse of linguistic diversity and recovering the 'primitive' language, as they called it, the language in which Adam had named every bird and beast at the Creation (Genesis 2:19–20). Many of these scholars were convinced that Adam had spoken Hebrew; some, that he had spoken Chinese; a few, that he had spoken a European vernacular—Dutch, for example, or Swedish.

As for Vico, his fascination with Plato's *Cratylus* was

already apparent in his *Ancient Wisdom of the Italians*. The *New Science* shows that he was also aware, or that he had become aware, of the recent debate on natural language, including the contribution made to it by another of his 'four authors', Bacon. Vico distinguished three main forms of communication, associated with his three ages. In the age of the gods, men communicated by means of ritual, 'mute religious acts or divine ceremonies', including the language of the hands. 'Among all nations the hand signified power.' Among the ancient Greeks, for example, 'those elected to power had it bestowed upon them by the laying of hands on their heads', while 'powers already bestowed were acclaimed by the raising of hands' (N2.1027). Early men also made use of sacred characters, or 'hieroglyphs', of which the Egyptian example is the most famous. In fact Vico cited not only Egyptian hieroglyphs at this point but also the picture writing of the Mexicans and the ideograms of the Chinese. This first form of language was natural, so he suggested, in the sense that both hieroglyphs and rituals had 'natural relations with the ideas they wish to signify'. In the age of the heroes, on the other hand, a conventionally symbolic language of images came into use (rather like the language of heraldry, which Vico discusses as an example of the recurrence of the heroic age in medieval times). Finally in the third age, that of men, came the invention of various alphabets.

Spoken language, according to Vico, went through a similar process of evolution from the natural to the conventional. It began with onomatopoeic sounds, another example of a natural relationship between the signifier and the thing signified. 'The philologians', Vico complained, 'have all accepted with an excess of good faith the view that in the vulgar languages meanings were fixed by convention. On the contrary, because of their natural origins, they must have had natural significations' (N2.444). In a process of ever-increasing abstraction, spoken languages developed interjections, pronouns, verbs, and so on. Vico also offered an explanation of the diversity of vernaculars in geographical and social terms. 'As the peoples have certainly by diversity of climates acquired different natures, from which has sprung as many different customs, so from their different natures and customs as many different languages have arisen' (N2.445).

There is much in this account which echoes ideas expressed in scholarly discussions of language in the sixteenth and seventeenth centuries. The point about the gradual development of linguistic diversity, for example, as opposed to the sudden catastrophe at the Tower of Babel, may be found in an essay by the English schoolmaster Thomas Hayne (1582–1645), an essay which Vico cites elsewhere. The parallel between the picture languages of the Egyptians, Chinese, and Mexicans had also been noticed by others long before Vico. In his theory of language, however, as in his theory of law, Vico's firm emphasis on the early history of mankind was an unusual one for its period. The origin and early development of languages would attract more attention in the second half of the eighteenth century, when Rousseau and Herder—among others—wrote essays on the subject.

Still more distinctive was Vico's stress on the concrete nature of primitive language and its analogies with the language of poets in other periods. Limited in vocabulary, the language of the first men was, according to Vico, all the more sublime in expression. This point was absolutely central to his system. The fact that 'the first peoples were poets' was, he claimed, the 'master key' of his new science. Poetry was older than prose. In the heroic age, men spoke in heroic verse. The ancient Roman law was 'a serious poem'. Roman schoolboys chanted the Twelve Tables as they learned them by heart. It is true that some of these points had been made before. One of Vico's older friends, the jurist Domenico Aulisio (1649–1717), had noted that the first laws of the people of Israel were in verse, while the idea that the first historians were the poets and indeed that poetry played a crucial part in the transition from savagery to civilization were Renaissance commonplaces. What makes Vico's theory distinctive is not so much his emphasis on verse as his emphasis on metaphor and on concrete // thought.

The same concern with concrete thought is the key—to use his own phrase—to Vico's still more celebrated theory of myth.

Even in ancient times, the Greek myths had been given a variety of interpretations. The traditional stories of the gods, as told by Homer and other poets, seemed too disrespectful to divinities to be taken literally. Already by the sixth century BC, these myths were seen by some commentators as allegories of natural processes, with the god Apollo, for example, standing for fire and Poseidon for water. In the fourth century BC, Euhemerus of Messina interpreted the myths not as allegories but as a distorted version of history, in which individuals distinguished for their achievements were remembered by posterity as divine: a view still described, in his honour, as 'Euhemerism'. The Stoic philosophers of Greece and Rome offered new allegorical interpretations of the myths, pointing this time to the moral lessons they contained. Medieval commentators took a similar view, which allowed them to find Christian meanings in pagan stories. At the Renaissance, the author of the best-known treatise on myth, Natale Conti (*c.*1520–82), combined the three main interpretations, the physical, the historical, and the moral. Building on Conti's foundations, Bacon, in his *Wisdom of* || *the Ancients*, offered, as we have seen (p. 21), some new political and physical interpretations of a number of Greek

43

myths. Alchemical ideas were also found in them. The myths were generally regarded as a secret language in which information had deliberately been hidden from 'the vulgar', a language which now awaited decoding by the learned.

However, the most significant innovation in the study of myth was the development, in the seventeenth century, of a comparative approach. Some scholars in the West now had sufficient knowledge of different oriental languages to become aware of the many similarities between the myths of the different cultures of the ancient Mediterranean—the Greeks, Hebrews, Egyptians, Syrians, Phoenicians, and others—in their accounts of creations, floods, miraculous births, and so on. These similarities were generally explained in terms of diffusion from a single source. Seventeenth-century scholars assumed that the Jews were the donor culture, and that similar myths found elsewhere were simply corruptions of these Jewish originals (occasionally justifying their assumption with the assertion that truth necessarily precedes falsehood).

For example, the French Protestant pastor Samuel Bochart (1599–1667), a man of extraordinary learning, argued that the story of Noah was a prototype on which a number of classical and other myths were modelled, while his pupil Pierre-Daniel Huet (1630–1721), later a Catholic bishop, suggested that the basic prototype was the story of Moses. Huet extended his basis of comparison well beyond Bochart's, and had some knowledge of the myths current in Canada, Peru, and Japan. As in the case of language theory, an increasing awareness of the world outside Europe was a stimulus to this new form of Euhemerism.

Vico knew the work of Bochart and Huet on myth, just as he knew of Bacon. All these scholars stimulated him into disagreement and the development of a new theory. His approach to myth (*mitologia* or *favole*, 'fables') was, like that of Bochart and Huet, a comparative one, which drew attention to the fact that 'every nation had its Hercules', its Jove, and so on, or their equivalents. However, Vico was no Euhemerist. Nor was he an allegorist like Bacon, at least not in the normal sense of the term 'allegory'. Just as he rejected the view that Jove, Hercules, and other gods and heroes had once been real men, so he refused to believe that they were mere literary devices, employed to express in coded form the teachings of philosophers on such subjects as ethics, physics, or politics. Vico considered the view that myths were a secret philosophical language to be an anachronism, much like the state of nature envisaged by the theorists of natural law. In both cases a modern rationality had mistakenly been imputed to early man.

Vico's positive suggestion was, as so often in his work, a synthesis of opposing approaches. He suggested that the heroes of mythology should be seen as 'poetic characters' (*caratteri poetici*). By using this somewhat idiosyncratic term (a play on words, since 'character' refers at once to a person and a form of communication), Vico was making the point that gods and heroes express abstract ideas in concrete form. They are the products of popular traditions, and not, as Bacon and others had thought, the creations of philosophers. Myths, then, are not distorted accounts of political events, as the Euhemerists had suggested, but true 'histories of customs'; not mere figures of speech but examples of the 'poetic logic' of the first men, in other words examples of a primitive, concrete, anthropomorphic mode of thought. Since this concrete mode of thought could be found everywhere in early times, and primitive customs too were similar to one another, gods and heroes of the kind the Romans named 'Jove' and 'Hercules' emerged spontaneously everywhere. Thus Vico saw no need for the elaborate diffusionist hypotheses of a Bochart or a Huet.

His account of the emergence of Jove, which so struck the imagination of James Joyce, was that when 'the sky fearfully rolled with thunder and flashed with lightning', early men were 'frightened and astonished by the great effect whose cause they did not know, and raised their eyes and became aware of the sky. And because in such a case the nature of the human mind leads it to attribute its own nature to the effect, and because in that state their nature was that of men all robust bodily strength, who expressed their very violent passions by shouting and grumbling, they pictured the sky to themselves as a great animated body, which in that aspect they called Jove . . . who meant to tell them something by the hiss of his bolt and the clap of his thunder' (N2.377). Here as elsewhere in the *New Science* we find a reminiscence of Lucretius, in this case of a famous passage describing the origin of religion; Vico's prose, incidentally, might be described as even more poetic than Lucretius's verse.

In a similar way to Jove, Hercules is presented in the *New Science* as the embodiment of an abstract idea, the performance of 'great labours under the demands of family necessities' (a curious contrast with the *Universal Law*, in which Hercules had figured as a 'poetic character' of the rise of the patron-client system). Different individuals had no doubt performed remarkable labours in the past—this concession Vico did make to the Euhemerists—but the individuals were conflated and assimilated to the prototype before they became part of the myth. This was the way in which the process of concrete thought worked. Again, 'Because of the first people's habit of thinking in poetic characters, their institutions and laws were all attributed by the Athenians to Solon, just as, by the Egyptians, all inventions useful to human civil life were attributed to Thrice-great Hermes' (N2.416). In other words, not only gods like Jove and demigods such as Hercules, but men such as Solon, Hermes Trismegistus, Romulus, the legendary founder of Rome, and the poet Homer were all interpreted by Vico as poetic characters, which men invented and at the same time believed: *fingunt simul creduntque*, as Tacitus wrote in a different context (Vico was always quoting his authors out of context, or using passages from them for purposes of his own). Whatever Vico had once owed to the hermetic tradition of late antiquity, revived at the Renaissance, he took his distance from it in the *New Science* by declaring Hermes himself to be a myth.

This striking contribution to the long debate over the meaning of myth was made, so it appears, without assistance from contemporary scholars, with two possible exceptions. Vico's friend Gianvicenzo Gravina (1664–1718) had published, in 1696, a *Discourse on Ancient Myths*, in which he described them as philosophy turned into images. In 1708 Gravina published a revised version of his discourse with a new title, *Poetic Reason*, which makes it sound close to Vico. In content, however, it remained closer to Bacon and to Renaissance tradition. Gravina argued, for instance, that in the *Iliad* Homer used the story of the Trojan War to represent 'all the customs of men'. He saw Homer as universal, while Vico's achievement was to see the *Iliad* and the *Odyssey* as time- and culture-bound. A second scholar known to Vico who had something to say about myth was Jean Le Clerc (above, p. 28), whose *Art of Criticism* discussed the use of myths as a historical source; but he produced no theory remotely like Vico's poetic characters.

Ideas rather closer to those of Vico had been or were being put forward by writers whose work he is unlikely to have known, except by report, because they wrote in English or French. Edward Stillingfleet (1635–99), bishop of Worcester, had, for example, suggested that Hermes Trismegistus might not have been a historical individual but 'an allegory' or even 'an Hieroglyphick', an idea which he did not develop but one which does not seem too remote from Vico's poetic characters. William Warburton

(1698–1779), bishop of Gloucester, discussed ritual, myth, and hieroglyphics as examples of concrete thought in early times when 'Language was yet too narrow, and the Minds of Men too undisciplin'd, to support only abstract Reasoning.' This remark comes from a book published in 1741, and it is enough to make one regret that the two men, who seem not to have heard of one another, never had a chance to meet and talk. Closer still to Vico's general line of argument was an essay *On the Origin of Fables* by the French philosopher Bernard de Fontenelle (1657–1757), an essay which was published in 1724 but had been written long before. Like Vico, Fontenelle adopted a comparative approach, and the myths of the American Indians reminded him of the Greeks. Like Vico again, he explained myth essentially in terms of anthropomorphism. 'The first men were extremely brutal', according to Fontenelle, and so their gods were necessarily brutal too. He quotes the same Lucretian example of the thunder and lightning leading men to imagine a god in the sky 'shooting arrows of fire'. Faced with parallels as close as these, it is hard to see Vico as a man born out of his time.

It is in the context of this discussion of concrete thought that we should place one of the discoveries of which Vico was most proud, his brilliant account of the nature of the Homeric poems. Book Three of the *New Science* bears the title, 'Discovery of the True Homer'. To make this claim intelligible, it will be necessary to take a brief look at earlier interpretations.

From ancient Greek times onwards, Homer's gods were criticized for their undignified behaviour, and a sense of unease with this lack of decorum encouraged allegorical interpretations of both the *Iliad* and the *Odyssey*. The travels of Odysseus, for example, were interpreted as an allegory of the journey through life of the human soul. An alternative explanation of the poet's lack of decorum was offered by the Greek critic Aristarchus in the second century BC. It was he who argued that Homer seemed undignified only because manners and customs had changed since his time. The allegorical interpretation of Homer's poems was the one which appealed to the Fathers of the Church, and later to the Renaissance humanists. By the seventeenth century, however, scholars were becoming conscious of two problems in Homer.

One was his portrayal of customs. The Homeric heroes shocked some critics because, like the gods, they seemed all too human, their manners coarse and crude, although they were supposed to be princes. On the other hand, certain scholars adopted the approach of Aristarchus and argued that the *Iliad* and the *Odyssey* were records of early customs and so valuable sources for Greek history. A book on the subject of *Homeric Antiquities* was published in 1677, the work of a Dutchman, Everard Feith.

The second Homeric problem which surfaced at this time was that of the transmission of the poems and of the changes which they might have undergone as they were handed down from one generation to the next. It was sometimes argued, notably by the French abbé D'Aubignac (1604–76), the Dutchman Perizonius (1651–1715), and the great classical scholar Richard Bentley (1662–1742), that Homer had not left his poems in their present form but had simply composed short songs which were later conflated to form the epics as we know them. Indeed, D'Aubignac even allowed himself to wonder whether Homer had ever existed.

Vico knew Feith's work, and possibly that of Perizonius, but he is unlikely to have come across the observations of Bentley and D'Aubignac, which had been made in books published in English and French. Yet his famous 'Discovery of the True Homer', which occupies the whole of the third book of the 1744 version of the *New Science*, reads

49

like an amplification and development of their subversive suggestions.

Vico had enormous admiration for the 'prince of poets', as he called Homer, and especially for the sublimity of his style. At the same time he was embarrassed, as some of his predecessors had been, by the lack of dignity of the heroes of the *Iliad* in particular. Achilles and Agamemnon, for example, are on occasion represented shouting drunken abuse at each other, 'calling each other dogs, as servants in popular comedy would scarcely do nowadays' (N2.782). Vico reconciled his embarrassment with his admiration by arguing that different periods have different standards of behaviour, and that Homer belonged to his age. The conduct of Achilles and Agamemnon, odd as it had come to seem to later generations, was in fact 'perfectly decorous' for that heroic (or barbarous) age. The *Iliad* and the *Odyssey* had to be seen as 'two great treasure stores of the customs of early Greece' (N2.902). It followed that Homer could not have intended the esoteric philosophical allegories which had been read into him by later commentators. Vico saw the Homeric poems, as he saw the Greek myths, as products of primitive thought. He was well aware of the importance of oral tradition in the transmission of the two epics. 'Homer left none of his poems in writing . . . The *rhapsodes* (singer of tales) went about the cities of Greece singing the books of Homer at fairs and festivals' (N2.849).

Vico also noted that the customs described in the *Odyssey* were more refined than those of the *Iliad*. This discrepancy forced him to the conclusion that 'the two poems were composed and compiled by various hands through successive ages' (N2.804). They were hundreds of years apart. So after years of writing about 'Homer' as a person, Vico shifted his position and suggested, as D'Aubignac had done, that the poet was a myth; not a historical individual, but rather 'an idea or a heroic character' of the

Greeks. He did not stand out from the Greek people. On the contrary, he was 'lost in the crowd' (N2.873, 882).

Vico's hypothesis about Homer derived much of its force—as the conjectures of D'Aubignac and Bentley did not—from the fact that it was embedded in a larger argument which concerned the history of language, the history of myth, and what the author liked to call the 'history of human ideas'. This last phrase was his way of referring to one of his greatest achievements. Translated into modern terms, thereby making it more intelligible at the price of some degree of anachronism, this achievement may be described as the discovery of concrete thought, or primitive mentality, or the savage mind. This discovery is a central theme of the *New Science*. There is nothing quite like it in the work of Vico's contemporaries or predecessors. However, as in the case of other great discoveries, it may be described as a systematization or as a making explicit of earlier insights. In the sixteenth century, for example, a number of writers had argued that the poets were the first historians and philosophers, without making it altogether clear why this should have been the case. In the seventeenth century, a tradition of interest in the history of ideas gradually became established. The term generally used for it was the 'history of philosophy', but in a sense wide enough to include what was called 'the philosophy of the barbarians'. There was a place in these histories of philosophy for the Brahmins and the Druids as well as for Plato and Aristotle. Vico's friend Valletta (above, p. 18) was one of the scholars who wrote a history of this kind, and Vico himself cited some of these seventeenth-century works in his *New Science*. However, his conception of the history of ideas was wider than theirs, just as it was wider than the history of learning which had been envisaged—as Vico well knew—by Francis Bacon. His idea of an idea was wide enough to include the history of practical reason, the

51

history of the assumptions revealed by human actions, the history of perception, and the history of 'common sense' (*senso comune*), defined by Vico as 'judgement without reflection, shared by an entire class, an entire people, an entire nation or the entire human race' (N2.142).

Others besides Vico had taken or were taking an interest in ideas in this broad sense. John Locke, for example, had suggested that children, savages, and illiterates are all incapable of abstract thought. Fontenelle (above, p. 48) had discussed primitive anthropomorphic thought in so far as it explained how myths originate. Montesquieu (above, p. 39), who shared a number of preoccupations with Vico, took a similar interest in the phenomenon of trial by battle in the Middle Ages, and offered a similar explanation in terms of a traditional mentality (*la manière de penser de nos pères*) though he did not generalize from this example as Vico did. A similar point might be made of the English critic Thomas Warton (1728–90), whose *History of English Poetry* discussed specific cases of what he called the medieval 'mode of thinking'. A German term with a similar meaning, *Denkungsart*, was coming into use at about the same time, in the middle of the eighteenth century, for much the same reasons.

Closest of all to Vico's approach was that employed in a study which appeared at much the same time as his, the *Customs of the American Savages Compared to the Customs of Early Times* (1724), by Jean-François Lafitau (1681–1746), a French Jesuit who had been a missionary in Canada and knew the customs of the Algonquins, Hurons, and Iroquois at first hand. He argued that these savages were not bestial (as many Westerners of the time supposed) but that on the contrary, they were highly intelligent, imaginative, and religious. He noted the similarities between their myths, beliefs, and customs and those of Europe in remote antiquity, as if the Indians had never emerged from the Homeric stage of civilization. He observed, for example, that both the ancient Greeks and the modern American Indians interpreted thunder as the voice of a god. Vico would surely have found this book fascinating, had he read it; but he would not have agreed with Lafitau's conventionally diffusionist hypothesis that the American Indians had migrated from Greece.

Vico's discussion of the history of mentalities (as it is often called today) was incomparably richer and more fully developed than any of the others just mentioned. He made a greater and more systematic effort to imagine 'how the first men . . . must have thought . . . the coarseness with which they must have given form to their thoughts and the disorderly way in which they must have connected them' (N.42). He drew an analogy between the mentality of children and that of adults in the 'childhood of the world', as he called it, a mentality which was both poorer and richer than that of adults and moderns. On the one hand it was impoverished so far as abstract concepts were concerned, 'incapable of abstracting forms and properties' (N2. 816), and lacking the concept of number, 'For the number system, because of its extreme abstractness, was the last thing to be grasped by the nations' (N2. 642). In compensation for these deficiencies, on the other hand, early thought was rich in imagination, in metaphor, and in personification. This was a 'poetic mode of thought' (*maniera poetica di pensare*), which naturally expressed itself in myth. It was marked by what would later be called fetishism, animism, and ethnocentrism. Vico did not use these terms, but he was well aware all the same of these three characteristics of archaic thought. Ethnocentrism he called 'the conceit of nations'. In the case of animism, what he wrote was that 'When men are ignorant of the natural causes producing things . . . they attribute their own nature to them' (N2. 180). As for fetishism, Vico wrote that 'men had a terrible

fear of the gods whom they themselves had created'
(N2. 916), another phrase reminiscent of Vico's
unacknowledged master, the Roman poet Lucretius.

It is worth adding that Vico's history of ideas, or modes
of thought, included the history of feelings. For example,
he believed that the impetuosity and the readiness to anger
of the Homeric heroes were an expression of their age, no
less than Homer's sublime language.

Until Vico, it had generally been assumed that human
nature was the same everywhere and at all times. This was,
roughly speaking, the view of the great Greek and Roman
historians and also that of the political theorists of the
Renaissance (notably Machiavelli), as well as that of Vico's
contemporaries. This statement needs to be qualified by
making reference to Aristotle's suggestion that there were
'slaves by nature' and also to the alternative, put forward
in sixteenth-century Spain, that certain peoples, such as the
American Indians, were 'nature's children', incapable of
self-government as of other forms of adult behaviour.
However, this somewhat ethnocentric awareness of the
geography of human nature does not seem to have been
accompanied by any consciousness of its history. Vico, on
the contrary, asserted that human nature had changed in
the course of time in quite fundamental ways, so that 'three
kinds of nature' corresponded to the three ages into which
his cycles are divided. It is time to look in more detail at his
views on the course of human history.

The course of history

Vico saw history as the gradual process of the humaniza-
tion of man. In the age before his three ages, there were the
giants, or *bestioni*, 'stupid, insensate, and horrible beasts'.
It has often been pointed out that this picture resembles
that painted by Lucretius. It is worth adding that a similar
picture can also be found in the early Christian writer

Eusebius, who declared that early men 'led a loose and wandering life like beasts', and also that some of them 'being in some small degree stirred by natural instinct' declared that divinities existed, like Vico's giants when they heard the thunder.

Then came the periods which Vico, in a characteristically poetic phrase, called the ages of the gods, heroes, and men. He had found this phrase, which is actually something of a classical commonplace, in the Greek historian Herodotus (*c*.484–420 BC), but it was one which—equally characteristically—he endowed with his own meaning. The age of the gods was simply the age when men 'thought everything was a god or was made or done by a god' (N2. 922). The age of heroes was heroic only in an ambiguous or ironic sense, since Vico defined it as an age when might was right. As we have seen (p. 50), he described the Homeric heroes as somewhat adolescent in their behaviour, touchy and violent. As for the heroic age of Rome, it was the time, he wrote, when the nobles treated the people with 'pitiless cruelty'. Vico seems to have used the terms 'heroic' and 'barbarian' as synonyms, perhaps to shock his readers into awareness that judgements on entire ages are not simple matters, if indeed such judgements are justifiable at all.

The third age, that of men, of reason, and of civilization, is the one of which Vico seems to approve most. However, this approval cannot have been whole-hearted, since he noted that this age's increasing command of abstraction, for example, was paid for by a decline in poetry, imagination, and the sense of the sublime.

It should be clear that Vico was not a typical man of the Enlightenment, looking down on earlier ages as times of 'darkness' and irrationality. Nor did he idealize primitive man as the Romantics were to do. He drew on the arguments of the scholars who despised the 'barbarians' and also on those who preferred the barbarians to the decadent

Romans, and he attempted to reconcile the two. Yet his position does not seem to have been a completely relativist one, like that of some ancient Greek sceptics, who argued (as he was aware) that it is impossible to judge whether one custom is better or worse than another. Vico appears to have adopted what it may be useful to describe as a 'semi-relativist' position. He suggested that certain good customs were universal (burial, marriage, and divine worship); but he denied that any one of the three ages could be said to be better or worse than another, because each had good and bad points which were impossible to separate. At the same time, he judged the goodness or badness of these specific features in accordance with some scale of values. He also referred to the 'acme' of a particular civilization, and described one point in the cycle—possibly his own time— as one of 'beasts made more inhuman by the barbarism of reflection than the first men had been by the barbarism of sense' (N2.1106). Exactly what he meant by this judgement remains obscure.

Vico's three ages are a 'cycle' in the sense that they form a necessary sequence which can be found in different parts of the globe and also in the sense that this sequence (*corso*) is followed by some kind of recurrence (*ricorso*). Whether or not the age of the gods has ever returned Vico did not say, but he did declare quite firmly that the heroic or barbarian age recurred in Europe after the decline of the Roman Empire. There was, he wrote, a return to 'fiefs', a return to hieroglyphic writing (he is thinking of heraldry), and a return to divine judgements (Vico compares medieval trials by battle or ordeal to the practices of early Roman times). However, unlike some seventeenth-century writers, including his admired Bacon, Vico does not discuss the process of transition from medieval to modern times—the roles played by money, gunpowder, printing, and so on.

The idea that history moves in cycles was no new one in

Vico's day. In ancient Greece and Rome, this view of the past had been the dominant one. A famous example is that of Polybius (*c*.203–*c*.120 BC), the Greek historian of the rise of Rome, who suggested that monarchy was naturally followed by aristocracy and aristocracy by democracy, and that when democracy went into decline, monarchy came round again. In the Middle Ages, cyclical views of this type generally gave way to the Judaeo-Christian 'linear' view of history as a movement towards a single goal, a 'consummation'. At the 'Renaissance'—the term itself implies a belief in cycles—the two conceptions of history coexisted and interacted, as they continued to do in succeeding centuries. As late as the eighteenth century, educated men were less likely to see their own 'enlightened' age as a time of irreversible progress than to regard it as the rising phase of a cycle which would be followed in due course by decline.

Vico's cycles were in most respects an intellectual construct of their time. However, two original features were built into his model. One was the stress on the different modes of thought dominant at different points in the cycle. The other was the unusually explicit account of the mechanics of change.

A classic cycle—whether it be found in a classical, Renaissance, or eighteenth-century writer—often begins with a description of a state of peace, which brings prosperity with it, followed by civilization, luxury, effeminacy, and so defeat at the hands of a poorer, more warlike, and more 'manly' society, which is then forced by its very success to go through the same sequence of changes as its late victim. Vico's early lecture on the sumptuous feasts of the Romans, with its argument that Rome was conquered by oriental luxury, fits into this general pattern. However, the mature Vico was not concerned with moral decline; as we have seen, his semi-relativist position made the term 'decline' virtually meaningless for him, and he did not

57

use it. What interested him was the study of major shifts in values and in modes of thought.

Vico's explanations of major changes in history were also rather different from those offered by his contemporaries and predecessors. They had to be, since he had a broader view than they of what was to be explained, and also because he came out strongly against the diffusionist approach to change which was orthodox in his day. As we have seen (p. 36) he did not accept the view that the Romans had derived their first code of laws, the Twelve Tables, from the Athenians; nor did he agree with the argument, common at the time, that similarities between the myths of different peoples showed that these myths had been derived from a common source, such as the Bible. According to Vico, it was by a process of spontaneous parallel development that each nation acquired its Jove, its Hercules, and so on. He had similar suggestions to make about linguistic change, replacing the traditional emphasis on the borrowing of words by a stress on the ways in which the language of a given people reflects its customs. Vico generalized his point and summed it up in the famous axiom that 'Uniform ideas originating among entire peoples unknown to each other must have a common ground of truth' (N2.144). Hence the importance to him of the argument that there were no societies of atheists and that all peoples practised religious rituals and had some kind of marriage ceremony and some form of burial of the dead.

This emphasis on development from within a society or culture, rather than on changes introduced from outside, is one of the central features of Vico's thought. One might say that he 'had to' believe in internal development because this kind of development comes about by necessity, and can therefore be described in the form of a system, as in the *New Science*, while the impact of external forces or the spread of influences is contingent and therefore resistant to systematization. His internalism is not only central to his thought but also one of its most original features. Some of the humanist lawyers of the Renaissance had, it is true, already suggested that changes in the law could usefully be interpreted in terms of development from within in response to changing needs, and that a legal system, like an individual, had its childhood, youth, maturity, and senility. However, it was Vico who extended this explanation to other kinds of change, generalizing it in this way at a time when diffusionism was dominant, so that he was swimming against the stream.

How then, according to Vico, did these all-important internal developments come about? He has a good deal to say on the subject, although it is not easy to turn his scattered observations into a completely coherent account. One of Vico's essential organizing concepts was the parallel just mentioned between the life of an individual and that of the human race in its three ages. 'Men at first feel without perceiving', runs a famous axiom; 'then they perceive with a troubled and agitated spirit, finally they reflect with a clear mind' (N2.218). However, another axiom states that 'The order of ideas must follow the order of institutions' (N2.238), followed by the statement that 'This was the order of human institutions: first the forests, after that the huts, then the villages, next the cities, and finally the academies' (N2.239), a sequence of five phases which does not fit his usual schema of beasts, gods, heroes and men. But the crucial question remains: what governs 'the order of institutions'?

It was not, as some French and Scottish thinkers, developing an idea of Grotius, would suggest in the 1750s, the changing 'mode of subsistence', which according to them produced a sequence of four stages of society: hunting, pastoral, agricultural, and commercial. Vico was not concerned with economic change—this is in fact one of the major weaknesses in his system. He was concerned with changes in people's minds—and this is one of his great strengths. He believed in the 'necessary harmony' of human institutions, in other words the necessary link between particular forms of culture and particular forms of society, a view which would later be described in terms of the 'spirit of the age'.

These links between culture and society were not planned by anyone. One of Vico's organizing concepts was the idea of unintended consequences, or, as it is sometimes and somewhat cumbrously labelled, the 'heterogenesis of ends'. One of the resounding statements of this principle occurs towards the end of the *New Science*: 'It is true that men have themselves made this world of nations . . . but this world without doubt has issued from a mind often diverse, at times quite contrary and always superior to the particular ends that men had proposed to themselves; which narrow ends, made means to serve wider ends, it has always employed to preserve the human race upon this earth.' This assertion of the importance of unintended consequences in history is presented, as so often in Vico, as a synthesis of two opposed views: 'That which did all this was mind, for men did it with intelligence; it was not fate, for they did it by choice; not chance, for the results of their so acting are perpetually the same' (N2.1108).

Elsewhere Vico wrote that legislation has created the strength, riches, and wisdom of particular societies 'out of ferocity, avarice, and ambition, the three vices which run throughout the human race' (N2.132)—in other words, 'private vices, public benefits', as the Dutch physician Bernard Mandeville (1670–1733) subtitled his *Fable of the Bees*, another of the works published in Vico's day which was relevant to his system but which he could scarcely have known, since it was written in English. Mandeville was thinking, like the Scottish economist Adam Smith (1723–90), of the 'invisible hand' of market forces. Vico, however, had a more traditional invisible hand in view, the hand of divine providence. But his notion of providence is not exactly a traditional one. It works through men rather than imposing its will on men, and it operates through long-term social processes rather than through events or individuals. Vico reduces individuals to symbols—even the individuals in whose historical existence he believed. For example, the sequence Achilles – Scipio – Caesar – Tiberius – Nero corresponded, according to him, to inevitable changes in the nature of peoples: 'first crude, then severe, then benign, then delicate, finally dissolute' (N2.242). In this sense even the emperor Nero is a 'poetic character'.

Vico both believes and disbelieves in providence in the traditional sense. He is on the frontier between the theological and the secular interpretation of history, and it is not always easy to see where he stands. Hence it may be useful to look more closely at a single instance of the general process by which, according to him, these unintended consequences work themselves out and major historical changes occur. The Roman example is one which he discussed in particular detail—indeed, it is the only example which he discussed at any length—in passages which are scattered through his book. These passages are sometimes inconsistent on points of detail, but they are compatible with one another so far as the main developments are concerned.

Vico's main point was that Roman history was marked by long and sometimes violent conflicts between two social groups, the patricians and the plebeians. These 'heroic struggles' were, according to him, a special case of a conflict which often recurs in history, the conflict between the rulers and the ruled, in which 'the plebeians always want to change the form of government, as in fact it is always they who change it', while 'the nobles always want to keep it as it is' (N2. 609). At first, in the age of heroes, the patricians were the sole rulers, for 'the first commonwealths in the world were born in a most severely aristocratic form' (N2. 582). They maintained themselves in power by keeping the laws in a secret language which no one else was allowed to learn. Their behaviour towards the plebeians, who held land from them by a form of feudal tenure, was 'haughty, avaricious, and cruel' (N2.272). They levied private taxes on the plebeians and on occasion they even shut them up in their private prisons.

This situation gradually changed, partly because the patricians set up, or allowed to be set up, two new institutions. The first was the *census*, or system of public taxation, which was to become 'the basis of popular liberty'. The second was the office of tribune of the people. The tribunes, 'by performing the functions for which they were created, that of protecting the natural liberty of the plebeians, were gradually led to secure for them the whole range of civil liberty as well' (N2.111). In other words, the plebeians first acquired 'freedom from' (that is, from arbitrary imprisonment), and then 'freedom to' (to participate in politics). Together with these institutional changes (whether as precondition or as consequence, Vico does not say) went changes in consciousness. The plebeians ceased regarding the patricians in a heroic light and 'finally . . . understood themselves to be of equal human nature with the nobles, and therefore insisted that they too should be taken into the civil orders of the cities' (N2.1101). The 'age of men' had arrived. The laws were now translated into the vernacular and so passed from the control of the patricians into that of the plebeians, who thus became sovereign. Aristocracy had been transformed into democracy. As Vico summed the process up at the end of the *New Science*: 'The reigning orders of nobles mean to abuse their lordly freedom over the plebeians, and they are obliged to submit to the laws which establish popular liberty' (N2.1108).

Exactly what did oblige the nobles to submit in this way remains obscure in Vico's account. However, in some passages he seems to imply that the crucial factor was their reverence for the laws, which had once been an instrument of patrician dominance but which they now permitted to limit their own freedom of action against the plebeians. We have seen (pp. 35 ff.) how Vico was concerned to show that law was the product of history. Here we may observe the converse: his insistence on the active role played by law in shaping history.

This account of Roman history in terms of the conflict between two classes will obviously have a Marxist ring to modern ears. The similarities are clear and close, despite Vico's lack of concern for the economic basis of class conflict. All the same, to describe Vico as 'anticipating' Marx is not a particularly useful way of describing the relationship between the two thinkers. It would be more illuminating to think of Marx as developing and making more precise a cluster of traditional ideas about social conflict, ideas which in some cases go back to the time of the Romans themselves (after all, it was they who coined the terms 'plebeian', 'proletarian', and even 'class'), while other elements in the cluster go back to the Renaissance, notably to Machiavelli. It was Machiavelli who argued, in his *Discourses on Livy*, that it was the conflict between patrician and plebeian which made the Roman commonwealth both free and powerful. Vico was well aware of this particular argument, disagreed with it, and went out of his way to answer it. He declared that 'the Roman Empire grew so great and endured so long', not for the reasons which Machiavelli had adduced, but because 'in its changes of constitution it made every effort to stand firm by its principles' (N2.1003). And yet, here as elsewhere in the

New Science, Vico was particularly indebted to an author he was concerned to refute. It seems that he needed the stimulus of an opinion which he found quite unacceptable in order to formulate his own.

Divine providence

Unlike Machiavelli, Vico repeatedly referred to divine providence. We have still to explore the question of divine intervention in history according to Vico, its extent and its modes, as well as the difference between sacred and profane history, as he saw it. It may be simpler to tackle the second problem first.

Vico's attitude to 'sacred history', by which he meant the history of the Jews as it is related in the Old Testament, is somewhat ambiguous. On the surface, it is true, it seems to be clear enough, for the *New Science* claims to be concerned only with the gentiles (*le genti*). Indeed, the title of the first edition of that book may be translated, 'The Principles of a New Science of the Nature of Nations, leading to the Discovery of the Principles of a New System of the Natural Law of the Gentiles'.

Vico made a sharp distinction between sacred and profane history. In the first place, sacred history was older. 'Sacred history is more ancient than all the most ancient profane histories that have come down to us' (N2.165). In the second place, the records kept by the Jews were more reliable than others: in the Old Testament they had 'accurately preserved their memories from the beginning of the world' (N2.54). The process by which change occurred in the two sectors was also different. 'Whereas the gentile nations had only the ordinary help of Providence, the Hebrews had extraordinary help from the true God' (N2.313). For example, 'The Hebrew religion was founded by the true God on the prohibition of the divination on which all the gentile nations arose' (N2.167). There was never any polytheistic phase among the Jews. Hence the human race was divided, in early times, into two groups, or even species, 'the one of giants, the other of men of normal stature; the former gentiles, the latter Hebrews' (N2.172). In other words, Vico's memorable description of the wild men wandering through the forests of the earth would seem to apply only to the early history of the gentiles, and the Jews would appear to have been exempted from the cycle of the three ages of gods, heroes, and men.

The point about the antiquity of the history of the Jews deserves further comment, for by making this assertion Vico was taking his stand in a long and important debate. From the Renaissance onwards, some scholars had claimed that the oldest civilization on earth was that of Egypt. They argued that the ancient Greeks had derived their gods from the Egyptians, that the Jews had derived many of their customs from the same source, and even that the Egyptian sage Hermes Trismegistus (above, p. 47) had been aware of the essential truths of Christianity, despite the fact that he was supposed to have lived long before Christ. The key witnesses adduced by these scholars were the texts attributed to Hermes himself, which were studied avidly in the sixteenth century, and also the testimony of Manetho, an Egyptian priest who lived in the third century BC and wrote a history in which he claimed that the civilization of the Egyptians went back more than 36,000 years.

In the seventeenth century, some Europeans urged the claims of the Chinese to have the oldest civilization on earth. For example, the Jesuit missionary Martino Martini (1614–61), who had studied the Chinese historical classics, calculated that the first Chinese emperor must have begun to reign in 2952 BC, or six hundred years before the Flood. The question whether the Flood was world-wide also gave rise to a lively controversy at about this time. One scholar,

Isaac de La Peyrère (1594–1676), argued not only that the
Flood had actually been confined to a relatively small part
of the earth but also that there had been men before Adam,
in other words that Adam was the ancestor of the Jews but
not of the whole human race, and that the Bible, far from
being universal, was no more than local history, the history
of one people. This belief in men before Adam was equally
unorthodox from Catholic, Protestant, and Jewish points
of view, but it seems to have gained some adherents. It was
one of the heresies of which some friends of Vico's had been
accused in 1691 (above, p. 15).

All these new opinions were attacked by the supporters
of tradition, who argued, for example, that the so-called
'ancient wisdom' of the Egyptians was not ancient at all,
that Manetho had been guilty of wild exaggeration when he
wrote of the 36,000 years of Egyptian history, and that the
books attributed to Hermes Trismegistus had actually been
composed in early Christian times, so that it was the
Egyptians who had borrowed from the Jews and Christians,
not the other way round. The claims to antiquity made on
behalf of the early Chinese emperors were also rejected.
Some scholars identified these emperors with Biblical
figures, such as Noah, just as Bochart and Huet had found
Biblical prototypes for classical and other myths.

One of the scholars who argued most strongly that the
history of the Jews went back further than that of the
Egyptians or Chinese was none other than Sir Isaac
Newton, who in fact spent much of his later life in the study
of chronological problems, using the evidence of astro-
nomy to help him synchronize the chronological systems
of different peoples. Newton's *Chronology of Ancient
Kingdoms Amended* was published in 1728, not long after
his death. The learned world had known for years that Sir
Isaac was working on this project, so that when Vico sent a
copy of his *New Science* to Newton (above, p. 28), his

homage may have been intended for the chronologist as well as for the natural philosopher.

For Vico agreed with Newton in rejecting the claims to antiquity made by and on behalf of the Egyptians and the Chinese. He was not very much concerned with the question whether the Egyptians influenced the Jews or the other way round because, as we have seen (p. 36), he rejected diffusionism. However, he was concerned to argue that sacred history was the most ancient history that has come down to us.

Vico was also concerned, as it was remarked earlier, to set sacred history apart from profane history. For example, he accepted the Biblical account of the Tower of Babel as valid for the history of the Jews, but he gave a quite different kind of explanation for the development of different languages among the gentile nations (above, p. 42). As previously noted, he claimed that the human race was in fact two races: the gentiles (descended from the giants) and the Jews. In a sense he was closer than he would have been prepared to admit to the position of La Peyrère, who had argued that Adam was the ancestor of only part of the human race; but Vico was also rendering unto Peter the things that are Peter's, and deliberately abstaining from involvement in matters of theology.

All the same, there are passages in the *New Science* where Vico appears to be undermining the very distinction he has been so careful to draw. Despite his remarks about the accuracy of the Old Testament as a record of Jewish history from the creation onwards, he begins the 'Hebrews' column of his chronological table with the Flood. His comparison of the law of Moses with Roman law and of the Bible with Homer does seem to place sacred and profane texts on the same level. One is left wondering whether in private Vico ever considered the Bible as a corpus of myth. As he well knew, this was what Spinoza had done.

Again, Vico's suggestion that the 'extraordinary' help of God had freed Christians from the cycle of the three ages is inconsistent with his description of the Middle Ages as a return of the age of heroes. The implication would seem to be that the principles of the new science apply to the whole of human history. In that case, Jewish history, like that of the gentiles, could be understood in terms of an 'ordinary' or impersonal providence. It would follow that, despite his claims to be putting forward a 'civil theology' and to be refuting the Epicureans and other 'atheists', Vico was asserting little more than the existence of an order behind the apparent chaos of events. He was once again offering a synthesis of opposites, in this case between the naturalist and the providentialist accounts of human development, between Lucretius (say) and Bossuet.

This brief account of Vico's views on law, language, myth, the course of history, and the role of providence may be summed up by saying that he combined traditional interests with new approaches. The novelty and the importance of his sytematically comparative approach are particularly worthy of emphasis. Systematic comparison was not a method which Vico invented, but he had only a few significant predecessors in this regard and he surpassed them in both sweep and subtlety. There was the Frenchman Jean Bodin (c.1530–96), whose work on history, law, and politics was well known to Vico; and Bochart, Huet, and other students of comparative mythology, whose diffusionism he rejected, like that of the Egyptologists—or Egyptomanes—of the seventeenth century. The comparisons between ancient Greeks and contemporary Amerindians made (apparently unknown to Vico) by Fontenelle and Lafitau were penetrating but narrower in scope than those made in the *New Science*, while the other masterpiece of comparative analysis, Montesquieu's *Spirit of the Laws*, was published twenty years after Vico.

Sources and methods

A striking feature of the *New Science*, at least for a modern reader, is that despite its grand comparative ambitions it is in fact based on sources which are almost all Western. Indeed, it is largely based on material from ancient Greece and Rome, particularly the latter. Vico was of course aware of other cultures, and he liked to illustrate his generalizations with brief exotic examples. The generalizations themselves, however, seem on the face of it to have been derived in the first instance from classical antiquity. For a man of his time, Vico took remarkably little interest in the history of Asia or America. He might be said to have discovered the 'savage mind', yet he scarcely looked at descriptions of contemporary savages, relying in their place on Homer and the account of the Germanic barbarian tribes given by Tacitus. He was openly contemptuous of many accounts of exotic places, which according to him included sensational but unreliable material in order to make the book sell: mere 'travellers' tales' (N2.334).

At this point it may be useful to list Vico's main references to the world beyond Europe: even an exhaustive list would not take up very much space. It is hardly surprising to find few references to Africa, for little was known by Europeans in Vico's day about the history of that continent. His own knowledge may be summed up in three propositions. The first is that the Ethiopians employed a kind of picture writing; the second, that the 'Kaffirs' of South Africa are said (falsely, according to Vico) to live without any knowledge of God; and the third, that the people of Guinea believe that the souls of the unburied remain restless on earth.

Vico noted a similar belief about the unburied among the indigenous inhabitants of Mexico, Peru, Virginia, and New England, a similarity which revealed 'what a great principle of humanity burial is' (N2.337). As mentioned previously, he held the view that burial, marriage, and worship were universal customs (they had to be universal because they were right, and they had to be right because they were universal—Vico does not seem to have been aware of the circularity of his argument). As in the case of the Kaffirs, he rejected *a priori* the notion expressed in some books that the inhabitants of Brazil and the Antilles were atheists. He was also aware of the scholarly controversy over the origin of the Americans, whether, for example, they had migrated from Europe or from Asia, but this question of diffusion did not interest him. On the other hand, he was fascinated by what he could learn about the picture writing of the Mexicans, and refers to it on several occasions. His discussion of the giants who wandered the earth in early times cites the example of the Patagonians, who were believed by Europeans in his time to be of gigantic stature. He illustrates his idea of the age of the gods with the fact that 'the American Indians . . . call gods all the things that surpass their small understanding' (N2.375).

Vico showed a rather greater interest in and knowledge of the cultures of the Far East, deriving his information mainly from accounts written by Jesuit missionaries. He made a passing reference to Siam, cited Japanese examples on more than one occasion, and took China still more seriously, although he did not accept the Chinese claim to great antiquity.

The Japanese, he suggested, still retained 'much of the heroic nature', for they were ferocious fighters and had 'a religion of fierce and terrible imagination with dreadful gods all armed with frightful weapons'. Like the Roman patricians of the heroic age, the Japanese nobles could not be 'persuaded that the plebeians have the same human nature as themselves' (N2. 1091).

Vico made references to China in eighteen of the 1,112

paragraphs into which modern editors have divided the *New Science*, although he did not include China in his comparative chronological table (did he have difficulty making up his mind about the dates of the Chinese dynasties?). He was fascinated by Chinese ideograms as yet another form of picture writing which had survived to his own day, although his account of the Chinese language is more than a little garbled (he wrote that the Chinese had '120,000 hieroglyphs', compared to a mere three hundred spoken words). He noted that in China, as in ancient Greece, a dragon was 'the ensign of the civil power', commenting that 'it is something to wonder at that two nations so distant from each other in space and time should think and express themselves in the same poetic manner' (N2.423).

Vico had relatively little to say about the world of Islam, about the Mughal, Persian, or even the Ottoman Empire, still a force to be reckoned with in his day. However, he did take considerable interest in the ancient Near East—in the Chaldeans, for example (twenty references in 1,112 paragraphs), in the Phoenicians (thirty references), and, above all, in the ancient Egyptians (ninety-five references)—despite his sceptical reaction to their claims to vast antiquity.

What was of particular interest to Vico in Egyptian culture was what he called the 'two great philological verities', which he found 'no less marvellous than their pyramids'. 'The first is narrated by Herodotus: that the Egyptians reduced all the preceding time of the world to three ages, the first that of the gods, the second that of the heroes, and the third that of men. The other . . . is that . . . through all that period three languages had been spoken: the first hieroglyphic, with sacred characters; the second symbolic, with heroic characters; the third epistolary, with characters agreed on by the people' (N2. 52). When, in the early nineteenth century, Egyptian hieroglyphics were at last decoded, it was discovered that they were not 'heroic emblems', as Vico and his humanist predecessors had thought, but ideograms. However, modern Egyptologists still refer to 'hieratic' and 'demotic' writing, so his social history of language may not have been too far off target.

Even in the case of Europe, Vico's historical knowledge was patchy. Despite his theory of the *ricorso*, he did not take a great interest in the Middle Ages. He had one advantage over most modern students of the period, in that he had spent much of his schooldays learning medieval philosophy, but this experience may not have increased his sympathy for medieval culture. As we have seen (p. 37), he knew a fair amount about the legal aspect of the feudal system. He was interested in the runic alphabet as in other systems of writing, and he studied the work of Scandinavian scholars on the 'Goths' in Sweden and elsewhere. He was aware of the special ethos of medieval knights, the code of chivalry, even if he was not particularly sympathetic to what he called 'the virtue of punctiliousness, on which the duellists of the returned barbarian times based their entire morality, and which gave rise to the proud laws, the lofty duties, and the vindictive satisfactions of the knights errant, of whom the romances sing' (N2.667). He knew something about the poetry of the troubadours, and he was a great admirer of Dante, the 'Tuscan Homer' as he called him. Indeed, a brief essay of Vico's survives which discusses the *Divine Comedy* as an example of 'sublime poetry': a modern editor of this essay has aptly entitled it the 'Discovery of the True Dante'.

All the same, this admiration for Dante was not enough to prevent Vico from characterizing the whole Middle Ages as an age of barbarism, without making any serious distinction between the seventh century (say) and the fourteenth. This lack of discrimination is the more surprising in that there was a movement among the scholars of the early eighteenth century in France, Italy, England, and Germany to rehabilitate the Middle Ages, particularly the later Middle Ages, instead of dismissing this period as one of barbarism and superstition. One of the leaders of this movement, the learned librarian Ludovico Muratori (1672–1750), was in friendly correspondence with Vico. The two men had common interests, including the significance of medieval trials by ordeal. Yet the *New Science* reveals no awareness of Muratori's fundamental work of revaluation, the *Italian Antiquities of the Middle Ages* (published 1738–42). Although Vico was still revising his great work, he seems to have stopped reading by this point. In so far as he achieved a sympathetic understanding of medieval mentalities, he did it alone, by intuition.

The focus of Vico's attention was on ancient Greece, from Homer to Plato, and, still more strongly, on ancient Rome, or more exactly, ancient Italy—for he was interested in the culture of the Etruscans and in that of the Greek-speaking inhabitants of his own region, the south. The presence of Roman history in the *New Science* is pervasive. The references are innumerable: to the mythical times of Romulus (mentioned in forty-two paragraphs), to the Twelve Tables (seventy-one paragraphs), to Cicero (thirty-nine), and to the Roman emperors anatomized so pitilessly by Tacitus. It is scarcely an exaggeration to claim that Vico derived his schema of human development from Rome in the first instance, and then discovered it in—or applied it to—other societies, whether or not he was aware that this was what he was doing.

His dismissal of the Middle Ages, his concern for classical antiquity and its exemplary character for him all suggest that Vico was at heart a Renaissance humanist, a suggestion confirmed by his frequent and favourable references to other humanists, from Petrarch to Lipsius. He was of course a late humanist, one of the last of the breed, aware of the Scientific Revolution of the seventeenth century and marked by the ideas of Descartes, even though he rejected and refuted them. All the same he was a man whose classical culture would have made him at home in Renaissance Italy, as in the Rome of Cicero and of Cicero's friend Varro (116–27 BC), a scholar whom Vico cited again and again. The fact that he knew his classics, particularly his Latin classics, so thoroughly made it easier for him to understand Rome from within.

By contrast, his knowledge of other cultures was derived from relatively few sources. He learned of ancient Egypt, for example, from a few classical sources, such as Herodotus, and a small number of works by seventeenth-century scholars. In a similar way, his picture of the Middle Ages was put together from a mere handful of modern studies or original texts. The texts did not, unfortunately, include the *Song of Roland*: it would be interesting to know whether Vico would have found in it the sublimity he attributed to Homer and Dante. He does in fact invoke the parallel with Homer in the case of 'the history of Bishop Turpin of Paris, full of all those fables of the heroes of France called paladins which were later to fill so many romances and poems' (N2.159). As for the wider world, Vico knew it only as it filtered through a small number of accounts by travellers and missionaries of the sixteenth and seventeenth centuries, such as the Spanish Jesuit José de Acosta (1540–1600) on Mexico and Peru, or the Italian Jesuit Martino Martini (1614–61) on China.

These sources do not add up to an impressive total. By the standards of his own age, or those of the great polymaths or 'polyhistors' of the seventeenth century, such as Bochart and Huet, Vico can hardly be considered a real scholar. However, he might have said with Hobbes that if he had read as much as other men, he would have known no more than they did. He had a remarkable gift for seeing the general in the particular, and so coming out with hypotheses which turned out to be fertile. His achievement is the more remarkable when one considers the uneven quality of the materials out of which his system was constructed. It is a salutary reminder to our more scientific age of the importance of historical imagination.

It is not only what Vico read that was significant, but how he read it. One of his most outstanding achievements was his technique of reading his sources between the lines, attending not only to what the author intended to say but also to his 'involuntary revelations' (as the great Italian historical novelist Alessandro Manzoni put it in his essay on Vico) about the culture and society of his time.

The obvious example illustrating this point is that of Homer. Earlier historians had read Homer as a source for the history of events, taking quite literally his account of the Trojan war, an account which happens to be quite unreliable. Vico, however, read Homer primarily as a source for the history of manners and beliefs. Homer provides a mass of information about Greek society in the heroic age—how men fought, how they feasted, how they held assemblies, and so on—information which is all the more reliable because it is introduced incidentally and almost unconsciously by the poet. The Homeric poems also reveal a mode of thought proper to the heroic age, a mode of thought of which the poet could not have been aware—for lack of self-consciousness is one of the leading characteristics of this mode of thought. It would be misleading to suggest that Vico was the first scholar to think of using Homer as a source for the history of ancient Greek customs and values: Feith's study has already been mentioned (p. 49). However, Vico developed this method of reading between the lines in a way which was uniquely thorough, self-conscious, and systematic. Modern historians of Homeric

Greece may disagree with some of Vico's conclusions (indeed, they frequently disagree with one another), but this does not alter the fact that Vico's work marks a milestone in historical method. Without this new method, which was taken further by nineteenth-century classicists such as Wolf (p. 4), social and cultural history as we know it would remain out of reach.

A crucial question remains. Did Vico piece his fragments together into a system with the aid of nothing but his native imagination? Did he not have a method?

In a sense, the whole *New Science* is one vast discourse on method, on 'principles', as the full title of the work reminds us. Yet the question, what Vico's method was, remains one which it is curiously difficult to answer.

It may be useful to distinguish the destructive from the constructive aspects of this method, looking at the destructive side first. Vico is not often considered as a sceptic—understandably enough, since he made a habit of attacking the sceptics, or 'pyrrhonists', as they were often called in his day, those who declared that nothing can be known for certain and that the wise man will therefore suspend judgement. So far as historical knowledge is concerned, however, Vico was more sceptical than most.

In the seventeenth century a number of beliefs about the remote past which had previously found wide acceptance among scholars were called into question. Serious doubts were raised about the authenticity of the texts attributed to 'Hermes Trismegistus', for example, that of certain treatises attributed to fathers of the Church, and that of certain pieces of classical literature. In the early eighteenth century, some scholars questioned the reliability of the generally accepted account of the early history of Rome, for which the principal source was Livy (59 BC–AD 17), who wrote several hundred years after these events had taken place. Some intellectuals, notably the French Protestant exile Pierre Bayle (1647–1706), went so far as to express a general scepticism about the possibility of historical knowledge.

Vico did not go so far as Bayle, another of those authors whom he cited only to refute while taking from them more than he was prepared to admit. However, he went considerably further than the seventeenth-century scholars whose doubts were limited to specific texts or facts. He suggested, for example, that until the second Punic War (218–201 BC), 'all that has come down to us from the ancient gentile nations . . . is most uncertain' (N2.118). With his gift for middle-range generalizations, Vico was able to specify certain patterns of historical error, two in particular: the 'conceit of nations' (*la boria delle nazioni*) and that of the scholars (*la boria de'dotti*).

These basic types of error may be summed up in two words, which Vico did not use, but which do not seem alien to his thought: ethnocentrism and anachronism. 'Every nation . . . has had the same conceit that it before all other nations invented the comforts of human life and that its remembered history goes back to the very beginning of the world. This axiom disposes at once of the proud claims of the Chaldaeans, Scythians, Egyptians, Chinese, to have been the first founders of the humanity of the ancient world' (N2. 125–6). As for the scholars, their conceit is 'that whatever they know is as old as the world. This axiom disposes of all the opinions of the scholars concerning the matchless wisdom of the ancients' (N2.127–8), and also of the opinions of Grotius and others about the origins of society (above, p. 34).

Once the board was swept clear of past errors, what was left? What were the constructive aspects of Vico's method? Taking up a phrase of Francis Bacon's, from the preface to his study of the wisdom of the ancients, Vico described his three ages of the gods, heroes, and men as respectively 'obscure', 'fabulous', and 'historical'. The age of men presented no essential problem, because it was generally well recorded. To deal with the problem of the 'fabulous' age, Vico developed his famous analysis of myths, showing (above, p. 43) that they revealed the history of customs, the history of society, and not (as the Euhemerists had thought) the history of events.

What of the 'obscure' age? Vico's solution to the problem of our knowledge of this most remote of the three ages is advanced in one of the most famous passages of the *New Science*, perhaps the best-known passage of all. 'In the night of thick darkness', he wrote, 'enveloping the earliest antiquity, so remote from ourselves, there shines the eternal and never failing light of a truth beyond all question: that the world of civil society has certainly been made by men, and that its principles are therefore to be found within the modifications of our own mind' (N2.331). This passage has been central to the debates over the nature and extent of Vico's originality and over the purpose and meaning of his *New Science*. The 'verum-factum principle', as it has come to be called, requires some comment and elucidation.

In putting forward this principle, Vico was turning Descartes on his head. Descartes had argued, in his *Discourse on Method*, that the study of history was a waste of time because we cannot acquire any accurate or certain knowledge of the human past, as we can (he claimed) of mathematics and the world of nature. Vico said just the opposite. His claim was that the principles of human society, the 'civil world' as he calls it, are actually more certain than the principles governing the natural world, because civil society is a human creation.

This distinction between our knowledge of nature, on the one hand, and on the other our knowledge of what is, collectively speaking, all our own work (laws and political institutions no less than works of art) had been drawn by a few classical, Renaissance, and seventeenth-century writers, including Hobbes, who once wrote that 'civil philosophy is demonstrable, because we make the commonwealth ourselves'. Vico was almost certainly aware of this tradition, or at least of some parts of it. However, his predecessors had made the distinction more or less in passing, while in Vico's case it was absolutely central to his thought. He placed the passage just quoted in a prominent place, at the very beginning of the section of the *New Science* entitled 'Principles'. It is therefore crucial to ascertain what the distinction meant for him, and in what sense he believed that 'the modifications of our own human minds', as he put it, provided the key to the history of the obscure early times, to what we now call 'pre-history'.

If we look more closely at what he says about this first age, we find that Vico frequently appeals to analogy, the analogy between the nature and development of the individual and the nature and development of society as a whole. Here are four well-known examples.

The most sublime labour of poetry is to give sense and passion to insensate things; and it is characteristic of children to take inanimate things in their hands and talk to them in play as if they were living persons. This philologico-philosophical axiom proves to us that in the world's childhood men were by nature sublime poets. (N2.186–7)

In children memory is most vigorous and imagination is therefore excessively vivid, for imagination is nothing but extended or compounded memory. This axiom is the explanation of the vividness of the poetic images the world had to form in its first childhood. (N2.211–12)

Languages must have begun with monosyllables, for in the present abundance of articulated words into which children are now born, they begin with monsyllables. (N2.231)

Last of all the authors of the languages formed the verbs, as we observe children expressing nouns and particles but leaving the verbs to be understood . . . Our assertion may be supported by a medical observation. There is a good man living among us who, after a severe apoplectic stroke, utters nouns but has completely forgotten verbs. (N2.453)

It was said of Adam Smith that he was interested in 'Theoretical or Conjectural History', supplying the lack of empirical facts about the behaviour of early men by 'considering in what manner they are likely to have proceeded, from the principles of their nature, and the circumstances of their external situation'. In a similar way, these generalizations about what would now be called 'developmental psychology' gave Vico a basis for what might be termed his 'conjectural history' of the age of the gods. The same axioms assisted him in formulating the interpretation of myth on which he based his reconstruction of the age of heroes.

An influential modern interpretation of Vico's thought presents him as an opponent of what we often call 'social science' and as a supporter of understanding from 'within', quoting the verum-factum principle in support of this view. However, as I understand this principle, it is not recommending the reconstruction of the past on the basis of empathy. Vico is not saying that the principles of the world of civil society are to be found within the mind of the historian who later studies them; he says that these principles are to be found in the modifications of the minds of a variety of people, including children, apoplectics, and American Indians. The changes or 'modifications' of which he speaks are accessible to public observation, to comparison, and to generalization.

Far from being an opponent, Vico was in fact a strong supporter of what he called 'the science of the civil world' (*la scienza del mondo civile*). Such a science is precisely what his book was intended to provide. It is of course crucial to understand exactly what Vico meant by this term *scienza*, and it has to be admitted that this Italian word was and is ambiguous. It can mean 'science' in our sense of the term, as in Galileo's *Discourse on Two New Sciences*, a book which may well have inspired Vico's own choice of title. On the other hand, *scienza* sometimes means no more than 'knowledge' in a wide and general sense. Still, the contexts in which Vico uses this particular term suggest that what he had in mind in most cases was the strong, precise meaning. In the title of his study and elsewhere in the text, *scienza* is associated with the term 'principles' (*princìpi*). The introductory statement about the seven main aspects of the book declares that one of these aspects is a statement of 'the principles of world history' (*princìpi della storia universale*). Another of the seven aspects of the *New Science* is a 'system of natural law' (*sistema del diritto universale*). Poetic Vico certainly is; chaotic he often seems (at least to those who approach him for the first time). Yet despite the apparent chaos and the real poetry, Vico is concerned to be systematic and even geometrical.

It is surely significant that Vico himself referred to his method as a geometrical one. 'Our science proceeds exactly as does geometry' (*questa scienza procede appunto come la geometria*—N2.349). Italian correspondents of Vico praised both his *Universal Law* and his *New Science* at the time of their publication for their geometrical method, a phrase reminiscent of the fashionable Descartes and of other seventeenth-century philosophers, notably Spinoza, who described his treatise on ethics as 'proved geometrically' (*ordine geometrico demonstrata*). In a work well known to Vico, the *Demonstration of the Gospel* (1679),

81

Pierre-Daniel Huet, bishop of Avranches, had tried to prove the truth of Christianity on the basis of a set of axioms.

How seriously, how literally are we to take Vico's reference to geometry? It cannot be reduced to a mere figure of speech, because the phrase is not isolated. The *New Science* does, after all, begin with a hundred and fourteen axioms. Some modern commentators on Vico do not believe that these axioms have anything to do with geometry, and suggest that they are simply aphorisms in which the main themes of the book are stated in lapidary form. An obvious parallel, indeed one which Vico himself was likely to have had in mind when he was writing, is that of Bacon, who stressed induction at the expense of deduction and would therefore have had no truck with axioms, yet presented his *Novum Organum* in the form of a hundred and eighty-two aphorisms. And yet there was an important difference between the two aphorists. Vico did claim to be producing axioms in the sense of propositions from which certain conclusions necessarily follow. He did claim, unlike Bacon, to be deductive. 'We will demonstrate', he wrote on more than one occasion, *dimostreremo*. He also referred to his 'proofs' and his 'corollaries'.

It is important to emphasize that Vico's axioms are more than rules of historical method. They do include such rules —for example, the famous warnings about the 'conceit of nations' and the 'conceit of scholars'—but they also include axioms of a very different kind. For Vico, history itself, as well as historiography, proceeds according to rule. There are 'principles of world history' waiting to be discovered. In other words, there is a pattern in the human past and this pattern, according to Vico, is not contingent but necessary. Hence he often uses the phrase 'must have' when referring to early times. The stages, for example, through which specific societies pass are, according to Vico, necessary ones. The age of heroes must follow the age of the gods, just as the sequence woods, huts, villages, cities, and academies is a necessary one.

These sequences are part of what Vico called his 'ideal eternal history' (*storia ideale eterna*), which is one of the seven aspects of the *New Science*. This platonic phrase could perhaps best be translated into twentieth-century English as 'ideal type', a term associated with the German sociologist Max Weber (1864–1920); or it could be rendered as 'model', in the sense in which economists and sociologists currently use that term. We have of course to be careful not to impute to Vico the ideas now associated with these technical terms, just as we have to remember that Vico's models, unlike many modern ones, were always dynamic or developmental. When he used the phrase 'ideal eternal history', Vico was claiming that certain major historical trends repeat themselves, thus giving rise to a sequence of broadly similar forms of political organization, law, mentality, literature, and so on. He did not claim that everything that happens is determined. On the contrary, he was vehement in his opposition to this idea of 'fate', as he called it, in the name of free will. He does not appear to have believed in the inevitability even of the basic sequence of forms, for he remarks at one point that Carthage, Capua, and Numantia 'failed to accomplish this course of human civil things' because of various obstacles (N2. 1088). How a sequence could be necessary yet not inevitable, Vico does not explain. If it was not inevitable, the sequence could at any rate be found in different parts of the world. It was normal, natural, and even providential.

If Vico's system was not, as has sometimes been claimed, purely inductive, it was not purely deductive either. It combined a concern for generalization with a taste for concrete detail, principles with facts, deduction with induction, and, as its creator liked to say, 'philosophy' with 'philology'. What was meant by 'philosophy' in this context seems reasonably clear: a system of principles. The term 'philology' is rather more difficult to gloss, because Vico was accustomed to use it in more than one sense.

In some passages of the *New Science*, 'philology' has its conventional meaning of the study of language, and the argument from philology means essentially the argument from etymology. Vico was fascinated by etymology. In his autobiography, he declared that he had once planned a 'universal etymology', one of the many schemes which were ultimately melted down and reshaped into the *New Science*. By modern standards his etymologies were unscientific, because he was not anything like rigorous enough in establishing the earliest form of a given word, and also because he was liable to allow his imagination to run away with him (this was, no doubt, part of his appeal for James Joyce). However, in these respects Vico was not much different from the seventeenth-century scholars (such as Bochart), or indeed the Greek and Roman scholars (such as Varro), whose work he often laid under contribution. It was only in the late eighteenth and early nineteenth centuries that linguists discovered the importance of Sanskrit and the relation of the 'Indo-European' languages to one another. What was most original and remains most stimulating in Vico's etymologies is his insight that the history of words, like the history of myths, offers valuable evidence of changing values and modes of thought. If in archaic Latin, for example, *fortus*, which is related to *fortis*, 'strong', had the meaning of 'good', this suggests that brute force was more highly prized in early Rome than it was later, when 'good' was rendered by another term, *bonus*. Thus the history of language provided valuable evidence for the early history of the human race.

In other passages of the *New Science*, however, Vico seems to have been using the term 'philology' rather differently, as a private shorthand for 'the humanities', or even for 'empirical evidence', including the evidence of material culture. Philology stood for induction as philosophy stood for deduction. When Vico suggested that the conclusions of philosophy and philology supported each other, he was claiming that human history illustrates certain principles and that it does not make sense without them; that there is an order underlying the variety of human customs. This was the central insight and the organizing principle of the famous book by Montesquieu, the *Spirit of the Laws*. In Vico's case too, the idea of the relationship between philosophy and philology came to him in the course of studying law, more exactly when he was reading Grotius on the law of nature. On one side there were the principles of justice, which are derived from God, and on the other there was their reflection, or distortion, in actual legal systems, which are the work of man.

It would seem, therefore, despite Vico's reference to geometry, that the method he employed in the *New Science* was closer to that of the jurists who, in ancient Rome and in early modern Europe, interpreted unwritten law by reducing it to rules or, rather, by revealing the rules which it implied. The logical status of the 'axioms' or 'dignities' which Vico placed at the beginning of the revised version of the *New Science* are not so close to Euclid as they are to the juristic rules of the ancient Romans.

In his autobiography, Vico remarked that, being born in Italy 'and not in Morocco', he became a scholar. One might add that, being born in Naples and not in London, he grew up a Catholic. He always claimed to be orthodox and he was—unlike his friend Valletta and his fellow-citizen Giannone—on good terms with the clergy. Some students of his work argue that despite his claims, Vico was unorthodox at heart and that in the *New Science* he quite deliberately presented his ideas in a disguised form, hoping to be read between the lines. This argument deserves at least a brief discussion.

As we have seen, Vico was attracted in his youth to the Epicurean philosophy of Lucretius, and some of his friends of that period were put on trial for heresy. The authors from whom he learned most, despite his conventional Catholic education, were either pagans (Plato and Tacitus) or Protestants (Bacon and Grotius), if indeed they were not unbelievers (as the orthodox of Vico's day described Machiavelli, Hobbes, Bayle, and Spinoza). As for the *New Science*, we have seen that it did not maintain the separation which its author had originally made between sacred and profane history, but suggested comparisons which might well raise doubts in the minds of readers concerning the nature of providence (which worked for the Gentiles as well as for the chosen people), or concerning the Bible (which appears as a not untypical product of a heroic age). A reader who applied Vico's axiom about the conceit of nations to the history of the Hebrews would have been led to conclusions like those of La Peyrère (above, p. 66), to the effect that the Bible was just a piece of local history.

However, none of these points proves either that Vico was a secret heretic or that he was deliberately ambiguous. He may have failed to be consistent simply because he was attracted by incompatible ideas. If doubts concerning providence were raised in the minds of readers of the *New Science*, in the eighteenth century or later, this may have been a consequence unintended by its author.

Vico's political ideas are even more elusive than his religion. A poor man in need of aristocratic patronage, he was prepared to write poems and orations in praise of the current viceroy, or to write against the unsuccessful conspirators of 1701—but later, when the regime had changed, to write their epitaphs in the flattering style which was the convention of the time.

Was he then 'apolitical', as Benedetto Croce once declared? There are passages in the *New Science* which suggest that their author had political opinions of his own, even if he did not care to make them too obvious. The occasional references to the Neapolitan nobility of the day seem to imply that Vico regarded them as a survival into the 'age of men' of the proud, cruel aristocracy of the 'age of heroes', a group which did not consider its social inferiors to be human beings at all. Himself a man of the people, Vico argued for the importance in history of popular wisdom, *sapienza volgare*. His view of the past had remarkably little place for so-called great men or great events. His book went even further in the direction of what we now call 'social history' than the *Civil History of Naples* written by his contemporary Pietro Giannone, whose work had attracted interest for this very reason in Britain and France. In this respect the *New Science* was an extremely unconventional work, subversive of historical conventions as it was of aristocratic values. It is understandable that the Neapolitan supporters of the French Revolution, who wished to abolish the feudal powers and privileges of the barons, should have admired Vico and attributed their own opinions to him.

Lack of evidence makes it as unwise as it is difficult to go any further in analysing Vico's politics. If he did have views on the current issues of his day, he is not known to have expressed them. He was a member of that group of professional men, lawyers for the most part, some of whom were challenging the power of the aristocracy of Naples in his day, but he was not himself politically active. It is possible that he saw the history of his own city, as he certainly saw that of ancient Rome, in terms of the conflict between patricians and plebeians. However, the *New Science* does not suggest that the plebeians were right or that one part of the historical cycle is superior to another. Indeed, one of Vico's achievements was to show that each age has—necessarily—its own virtues and its own vices. In this respect he was as different from his successors, the historians who stressed progress, as he was from his predecessors, who emphasized decline.

Given that the *New Science* was in places obscure and ambiguous, and also that it avoided simple moral judgements, it was almost inevitable that later generations would understand the book in a variety of ways. Some of these interpretations have been discussed already. Others form the subject of the next chapter.

4 Vico and posterity

For a long time Vico went largely unappreciated. Newton, Montesquieu, Rousseau, Wolf, and Niebuhr are among the intellectuals who seem to have been ignorant of Vico's work at the time when they were coming to think along similar lines. Indeed, it has been observed that Vico finally became famous at the very moment when posterity had nothing more to learn from him. The observation is a penetrating one, but it will appear to be somewhat exaggerated if we look at the nineteenth- and twentieth-century thinkers who were attracted by Vico's ideas and in some cases called themselves his disciples.

At this point it should at last be possible to describe what it was that they saw in Vico. Of course they did not all see him in the same way, and this diversity makes it necessary to discuss whether or not they misunderstood what he was saying. The difficulty here is that describing a particular reading of the *New Science*—or any other text—as a misreading implies that there are criteria by which another reading may be judged to be 'correct'; but there are no uncontroversial criteria of validity in interpretation.

Indeed, there is a major conflict raging in our time over precisely this question of the 'reception' of authors and their texts by readers at the time and later. Simplifying the issues somewhat, we may distinguish two main schools or parties. On one side there are the scholars who argue that a text does have one definite meaning, the one intended by the author, and that new readings are simply wrong, because they are anachronistic, in other words projections of modern attitudes on to the past. On the other side there are the critics who suggest that texts have multiple rather than single meanings, including meanings of which no one but the author was aware at the time, and sometimes not even the author. In other words, they think of texts as in some sense containing latent meanings which time makes manifest, potential meanings which are gradually realized. If one were to ask why the first readers, or even the author, did not notice these meanings, the answer might be that in any one culture or period certain ideas are screened out, or repressed, because they are subversive or fail to fit the expectations or the mental schemata of the readers of that period. When the schemata change, the text looks different. Its meaning may be described as the sum of its actual (or even its possible) interpretations, or, in a more moderate version of the claim, the sum of those interpretations which have acquired a certain measure of acceptance.

Historians have traditionally tended to be more sympathetic to the first of these two options, but the second view is not necessarily unhistorical. It is simply concerned with a different kind of history, the history of the text from the point of view of the consumer rather than the producer, the reader rather than the author. All we can say is that supporters of the second approach run a greater risk of being unhistorical or anachronistic (while supporters of the first view run the risk of falling into a narrow literal-mindedness).

However, anyone who assumes that our own age possesses the 'master key' to the 'discovery of the true Vico' would do well to remember that we (the readers of this book no less than its author) are as much creatures of our time as our predecessors were of theirs, suffering the limitations as well as enjoying the advantages of standing at this particular point in time. We are as likely as our predecessors to project ourselves and our own values on to the past instead of seizing it and comprehending it in all its otherness as Vico tried to comprehend the first men.

Whichever party is right, or even if it is impossible to declare one party 'right' and the other 'wrong' in this dispute over interpretation (one dreams of going beyond these positions, of making a synthesis, as Vico himself might have done), the history of the changing responses to the *New Science* has something important to teach us. As has already been remarked, it is a book which is unusually open to diverse interpretations. Just as Vico read his predecessors in his own idiosyncratic way, using them to stimulate his own ideas and then attributing these ideas to them, so he has in return been unusually subject himself to this process of creative misinterpretation.

To discuss the interpretations of Vico offered by all the philosophers, poets, historians, lawyers, and others mentioned in the first chapter would be a major undertaking. It would seem to be more useful to discuss a small number of interpretations in relative detail. Two cases have been chosen: the romantic view of Vico, exemplified by Michelet, and the so-called 'historicist' view associated with Croce, Meinecke, and Collingwood. The final paragraphs will return to the question of Vico's significance for our own time.

Before he ever read a word of Vico, Michelet had planned a study of the vocabulary of different languages as an indicator of national character. It was as a result of this interest that he came across *The Ancient Wisdom of the Italians*, with which his project turned out to have much in common. Michelet then turned to the *New Science*, in the hope that it would be of relevance to his 'history of humanity', which was to deal not only with 'external' events but also with the character of peoples. It was then that he was, as he put it in his grandiloquent way, 'seized by a frenzy caught from Vico'. What impressed him most in the *New Science* was the 'great idea' that what mattered in history was not the individual event, fact, or person, but the

91

anonymous story of social evolution, the true history of humanity. As he confided to his journal in 1824, 'Vico. Effort, infernal shades, grandeur, the Golden Bough'. This cryptic phrase suggests that Michelet felt that it was his encounter with Vico which allowed him to understand the past and 'resurrect' the world of the dead, just as possession of the golden bough had allowed Aeneas to descend into the underworld and to question the shades. It was, incidentally, Michelet who made the point that Vico had been isolated and misunderstood in his own day because he had been born too early. 'He had forgotten the language of the past and could only speak that of the future.' The achievement of this 'solitary genius' was that he 'founded the philosophy of history'.

It would be perverse to deny that these two poetic historians had much in common, or that Michelet was responding to ideas which were really present in the text of the *New Science*, notably the idea that history is essentially concerned with long-term changes in ways of life and modes of thought rather than with the deeds of individuals. All the same, Vico might well have been surprised had he heard Michelet's praise of him as the founder of the philosophy of history, and not simply because this phrase had not yet been coined in his day. As he explained to readers of his *New Science*, the book has seven 'principal aspects'. It is not only a 'history of human ideas' and 'an ideal eternal history traversed in time by the histories of all nations' (N2.391–3), aspects which Michelet's phrase might be said to have summarized, but it is also intended to be a 'system of the natural law of nations', a 'philosophy of authority', and a 'philosophical criticism', aspects which Michelet ignored. In short, Michelet selected from Vico's work only what harmonized with, or echoed, his own preoccupations. It was this romanticized but somewhat reduced Vico whose fame he spread in France, all the more successfully because

92

of the growing interest in the philosophy of history of the German philosopher Hegel, to whom Vico was sometimes compared.

In the twentieth century, Croce has done for Vico very much what Michelet had done for him in the nineteenth. That is, he made Vico more widely known by presenting him as a modern, focusing on certain features of his thought but omitting others and thus turning him into a 'historicist'. 'Historicism' (*storicismo*), in the sense in which Croce used this rather ambiguous term, may be defined as the doctrine that historical events are unique, not subject to general laws, that no two instances are comparable, and that each historical period should be interpreted in terms of its own ideas and principles and—important addition—no others. The emphasis on the principles peculiar to a given period is not unlike Hegel's 'spirit of the age', and Croce was in fact a great admirer of Hegel. However, the doctrine of the uniqueness of historical events was reformulated in the late nineteenth century in reaction against the claims of the 'positivists' (above, p. 6) to study behaviour in a 'scientific' manner. Dilthey, for example, argued that the humanities (*Geisteswissenschaften*, 'cultural studies', was his term), employ a method which is quite different from that of the natural sciences (*Naturwissenschaften*), because humanists understand 'mind' or 'culture' (*Geist*) from within, by 'empathy', rather than merely explaining from outside, as scientists do. Dilthey was involved in a lively controversy with the founders of experimental psychology because he claimed that psychology depended on introspection, not on measurement. A philosopher of the same school as Dilthey, Wilhelm Windelband (1848–1915), emphasized the difference between the 'idiographic' studies, such as history, studies which are concerned with individual men or individual events, and the 'nomothetic' sciences, which are concerned with the formulation of general laws.

Himself in revolt against positivism, Croce was extremely interested in the ideas of these German philosophers, but he believed, as he told Windelband, that they had been anticipated by Vico in the course of his discussion of the verum-factum principle (p. 78). Croce was struck by the analogy between Vico's resistance to the Cartesian 'mechanical philosophy' of his own day and the historicists' resistance to positivism two centuries later. Indeed, he treated the two movements of resistance as if they were one. Ironically enough, Croce was being unhistoricist in presenting Vico in this way. Like Michelet, he was led by his enthusiasm for Vico to ignore aspects of the *New Science* with which he was out of sympathy, notably Vico's concern for comparison, for generalization, and for system. These were of course the very aspects of Vico which had had most appeal to the positivists a generation before Croce.

In the great debate over method which took place in the late nineteenth century, both sides could equally well have cited Vico in their support, the historicists because he stressed understanding from within and the positivists because he emphasized the existence of laws of social development. Indeed, it might well be argued that Vico's intellectual strength was precisely that he joined together what the positivists and the historicists put asunder.

In any case Croce's real affinity with some aspects of Vico's thought, an affinity which made him susceptible to its influence, blinded him to the rest. His interpretation was not wrong as far as it went, any more than Michelet's had been, but it left too much out. One might say that Croce's passionate belief in the relevance of Vico to the early twentieth century made him see parts of the *New Science* with great clarity but prevented him from seeing it as a whole.

The moral of this story for our own time will be obvious enough. Like Michelet and Croce, many people today feel an affinity with Vico, who seems to be addressing some topical issues. His interest in the savage mind seems to anticipate the anthropologist Claude Lévi-Strauss, while his concern with the language and thought of the child is reminiscent of the developmental psychologist Jean Piaget. His interest in mentalities or modes of thought and in their relationship to literacy or illiteracy also seems to prefigure current debates in both social anthropology and social history. It is understandable that some of his modern admirers claim that 'we live in a Vichian age'. However, at this point the examples of Michelet and Croce may serve to put us on our guard. We will not understand Vico if we think of him as a Lévi-Strauss or a Piaget in eighteenth-century costume. In saying this I do not mean to deny that there is any analogy between the ideas of Vico and Lévi-Strauss on the savage mind, or between the ideas of Vico and Piaget on the way in which children think; the point is simply to stress that these analogies are never more than partial. Vico's relevance to us is no less great for being indirect.

The *New Science* remains well worth studying, partly because it is a great imaginative achievement, like the poems of Homer and Dante, and partly because it is a seminal work, in the sense that it has again and again shown its capacity to sow fruitful seeds in the imagination of its readers. Vico's remarkable gift for seeing unsuspected connections has not lost its power to stimulate and to inspire.

Further reading

The standard edition of Vico's works in Italian is the one edited by Benedetto Croce and Fausto Nicolini (8 volumes in 11, Bari, 1914–42). There are more recent Italian editions of the *New Science*, and a concordance to its first edition (ed. A. Dura, Rome, 1981).

In English the *Autobiography* (trans. Thomas Bergin and Max Fisch, Cornell University Press, 1944) makes an attractive starting-point for the study of Vico. The same translators have produced an equally reliable version of the 1744 edition of the *New Science* (Cornell University Press, 1948; revised edition, 1968; abridged edition, 1961). Also available in English is the 1708 oration, *On the Study Methods of Our Time* (trans. Elio Gianturco, Indianapolis, 1965). *Vico: Selected Writings* (ed. and trans. Leo Pompa, Cambridge, 1982) contains selections from the 1708 oration and from the *Ancient Wisdom of the Italians* as well as from the 1725 version of the *New Science*.

There is no lack of studies of Vico, although some of the most valuable are available only in Italian. In English there are three volumes of collected studies, uneven in quality but each containing some important contributions: *G. B. Vico*, ed. Giorgio Tagliacozzo and Hayden White (Baltimore, 1969); *G. B. Vico's Science of Humanity*, ed. Giorgio Tagliacozzo and D. P. Verene (Baltimore and London, 1976); and *Vico: Past and Present*, ed. Giorgio Tagliacozzo (Atlantic Highlands, 1981). Of more specialized interest is *Vico and Marx*, ed. Giorgio Tagliacozzo (Atlantic Highlands, 1983).

General studies of Vico include Isaiah Berlin's *Vico and*

Herder (London, 1976): it is written with the author's customary brilliance but remains essentially within the Croce tradition.

There are many valuable studies of Vico's development. Fausto Nicolini, *La giovinezza di G. B. Vico* (Bari, 1932), and Nicola Badaloni, *Introduzione a G. B. Vico* (Milan, 1961), provide detailed information on his intellectual milieu. On his reading, Guido Fassò, *I quattro autori di Vico* (Milan, 1949); Enrico de Mas, 'Vico's Four Authors', in Tagliacozzo and White; Donald Kelley, 'Vico's Road', in Tagliacozzo and Verene; Bruce Haddock, 'Vico on Political Wisdom', *European Studies Review* 8, 1978; and Paolo Rossi, *Le sterminate antichità* (Pisa, 1971). The differences between the 1725 and the 1744 editions of the *New Science* receive a perceptive analysis from a literary point of view in Mario Fubini, *Stile e umanità di G. B. Vico* (second ed., Milan–Naples, 1965).

Vico and law. See Kelley, 'Vico's Road', cited above, and Max Fisch, 'Vico on Roman Law' in *Essays Presented to G. H. Sabine* (Ithaca, 1948).

Vico and language. Robert Hall. 'Vico and Linguistic Theory', *Italica* 18, 1941, emphasizes his debt to the humanist tradition. Hayden White, 'The Tropics of History: the Deep Structure of the *New Science*', in Tagliacozzo and Verene, suggests that Vico used this theory of linguistic transformation as a model for his history of consciousness.

Vico and myth. Frank Manuel, *The Eighteenth Century Confronts the Gods* (Cambridge, Mass., 1959), puts Vico's views into the context of their time. See also David Bidney, 'Vico's New Science of Myth', in Tagliacozzo and White, and Gianfrancesco Cantelli, 'Myth and Language in Vico', in Tagliacozzo and Verene.

Further reading

The course of history. Arnaldo Momigliano, 'Vico's *Scienza Nuova*: Roman "Bestioni" and Roman "Eroi" ' in his *Essays in Ancient and Modern Historiography* (Oxford, 1977), chapter 15.

Vico's method. Roberto Mondolfo, *Il verum-factum prima di Vico* (Naples, 1969); Leo Pompa, *Vico* (Cambridge, 1975); William Walsh, 'The Logical Status of Vico's Ideal Eternal History' in Tagliacozzo and Verene; Bruce Haddock, 'Vico's Discovery of the True Homer', *Journal of the History of Ideas* 40, 1979.

Vico's politics. Frederick Vaughan, *The Political Philosophy of G. B. Vico* (The Hague, 1972); Giovanni Giarrizzo, 'La politica di Vico' in his *Vico* (Naples, 1981); Jeffrey Barnouw, 'The Critique of Classical Republicanism in Vico's *New Science*', *Clio* 9, 1980.

Vico and posterity. Edmund Wilson, *To the Finland Station* (New York, 1940), ch. 1, 'Michelet discovers Vico'; Pietro Piovani, 'Vico without Hegel', in Tagliacozzo and White; Hayden White, 'What is Living and What is Dead in Croce's Criticism of Vico', in Tagliacozzo and White.

R. Crease, *Vico in English* (Atlantic Highlands, 1978), is a bibliography of writings both by and about Vico.

Index